COMPELLING BELIEF

THE CULTURE OF
AMERICAN SCHOOLING

COMPELLING
BELIEF

The Culture of
American Schooling

STEPHEN ARONS

New Press

McGRAW-HILL BOOK COMPANY

New York St. Louis San Francisco
Hamburg Mexico Toronto

For Nancy, Rebecca, and Ben

ISBN 0-07-002326-3

LIBRARY OF CONGRESS CATALOGING IN PUBLICATION DATA

Arons, Stephen.
   Compelling belief.
   1. Academic freedom—United States.
2. Education—United States.   3. Free schools—
United States.   4. Education and state—United
States.   I. Title
LC72.2.A76   379.73   82-7798
ISBN 0-07-002326-3   AACR2

Book design by Chris Simon

Contents

Acknowledgments

Part of the research and writing leading to this book was supported by the National Institute of Education (NIE-G-79-0161) and by the Liberty Fund, Inc. I am especially grateful to Kenneth Templeton, Jr., for his generous and unwavering support, and to William Johnson and George Pearson, whose confidence in the importance of this inquiry were crucial to its beginning. I am also indebted to my colleagues in the Department of Legal Studies at the University of Massachusetts at Amherst, not only for supporting a year's sabbatical for research and writing, but for teaching me, by example, the breadth and humanity that can be brought to an interdisciplinary inquiry in law and culture.

Those who have my greatest thanks are the parents and children, teachers, school officials, attorneys, ministers, and countless community members who spent so much time talking to me and whose openness about social conflict and about personal convictions are the basis of this book. I hope I have honored their openness with fair discussion of their beliefs and responsibilities and with respect for their confidences and anonymity where appropriate. My greatest intellectual debt is to Charles Lawrence III, whose ability to combine questions, support, and criticism have always sharpened my thinking and intensified my commitment.

Andy Sinauer and Mel Zerman provided advice, information, and friendship without which this book might never have seen the light of day. I was the beneficiary of research assistance from Julia Heller and Meg Caulmare. For typing various drafts of the manuscript, thanks to Norma Wasser, Argie Staples, Susan Munro, and to the untiring and totally competent Maggie Way. To my editor, Alfred Prettyman, I am indebted for help in making this a better book.

Finally, for her endless support, unflinching criticism, continual conversation, and constructive comments—and for tolerating the disruption of her own career while I traveled and wrote—I thank Nancy Felder Arons.

Chapter 1, "Book Burning in Warsaw," and Chapter 7, "Is Educating Your Own Child a Crime?" appeared in shortened and edited form in the *Saturday Review*.

Introduction

> We have the paradox of a society in which the capacity to do is
> developed beyond any historical example but in which no one
> is certain what is worth doing.
>
> —Murray Murphey

The raw material from which this book is made is
conflict—corrosive, irreconcilable, and proliferating conflict
between government and family. When the interviewing of
parents and public officials and the examination of disputes
began, this work was meant merely to produce a series of
case studies and an analysis of their legal significance. As the
inquiry proceeded, however, it became clear that sifting
through school conflict was but one way of uncovering a
more general struggle for meaning; one between the forces of
private dissent and the agents of public orthodoxy. From the
conflicts chosen and reported here, four themes emerged to
describe the intent of the book.

This book is about the stifling of dissent by an institution
widely acclaimed as the bulwark of democracy in America. It
may be no surprise to late twentieth-century cynics that institutions eventually destroy the goals they were meant to
achieve; but it is nevertheless a paradox that a society should
repress intellectual freedom with the institution of education.

This book is also about the perception of some families
that the assumptions of American culture no longer explain

the past or predict the future. After discussions with dozens of families, it seemed that no sketch of family/school conflict would be accurate without mention of the fear of parents that their children were growing up amidst a rubble of collapsed cultural meanings and dysfunctional social values.

These two themes join to form a third: the need to restructure the system of compulsory public education if it and freedom of belief and expression are to survive a time of cultural uncertainty and transition. The maintenance of an outmoded structure of education is in large part responsible for the conflicts reported here. In them can be seen what happens to the definition, revitalization, and transmission of values in society when a large part of the child-rearing function is handed over to a politically controlled, majority-oriented, and bureaucratically organized system of schools.

Finally, this book is about the apparent inability of the law to incorporate the reality of family life and conflict into its decisions, when to do so would contradict prevailing ideologies or threaten important institutional interests. Though we might wish our legal system were capable of creating community cohesion by resolving conflict and though we might intend schooling to breed that cohesion by socializing the next generation, the intersection of law and education in these cases has created conflict rather than consensus. In these cases the law has fallen short because of its failure to comprehend the significance of most family/school conflicts.

In spite of these disturbing themes, the tone of what follows is essentially up-beat, for it describes how the struggle to understand and affect culture and politics transforms personal acquiescence into public action. The confusion and alienation these families feel have not paralyzed them or taught them passivity but have instead increased their sense of engagement with life and released their energy as dissent. As expected, the values expressed and fought for by these dissidents are, more often than not, unattractive, wrong-headed, and contrary to the accepted wisdom of the majority. Dissent, by definition, is unpopular. Yet they have acted on conscience, have shown clear commitment to their children, and have expressed fears common to many of us. It is, therefore, inappropriate for the majority to dismiss the dissidents as deranged or to congratulate itself that lack of involvement in school politics is healthy.

The structure of this book is simple. Each of the first three parts reports and comments on a different form of conflict between families and schools; the fourth part analyzes these conflicts from the perspective of liberties guaranteed by the First Amendment. Part One deals with censorship in the public schools, the battles of competing groups of parents for control of curriculum and libraries. Part Two deals with home education: individualism at its height and the ultimate challenge to institutional life and institutionalized schooling. Part Three examines government control of private schools. Its theme is group dissent—the struggle of subcultures against the imposition by government of unwanted values in school policy.

Part Four summarizes the analysis and then argues that all of these conflicts are made inevitable and unending by the peculiar structure of schooling in America. It is contended that freedom of expression and the vitality of dissent are threatened by a system in which private choices based upon conscience and belief are subject to the approval of the majority. Ultimately it is contended that the present structure of public education is unconstitutional because the primary victims of the unequal distribution of liberty in education are the poor, working people and racial minorities.

The conflicts reported here involve values, beliefs, and world views about which people are not inclined to compromise under threat of compulsion. The importance of such beliefs to social life and personal identity is paramount; and that is why the battles reported here are so pitched. The conflicts dealt with in this book give rise to situations whose destructiveness results from the refusal of the disputants to compromise their beliefs, from the inappropriateness of using the political process to decide matters of conscience, and from the fact that the freedom to differ on basic matters of belief has itself become a matter of principle for dissenting families.

Of course not all conflict over world views and beliefs—no matter how tense in its public appearance—is necessarily irreconcilable. Where value conflict can be resolved, the disputants and the culture gain stability and cohesion, and the law reaches its highest function. The constructive use of school conflict is treated in Sara Lawrence Lightfoot's *Worlds Apart*:

> It is critical . . . that we distinguish between creative conflict and negative dissonance between family and school. The former is inevitable in changing society and adaptive to the development and socialization of children. The latter is dysfunctional to child growth and acculturation and degrading to families, communities and culture . . . Conflict is potentially constructive as a way of clarifying and resolving differences in culture and ideology between families and schools . . .

The destructive struggles over world view and belief discussed here are currently alive; but they have antecedents in the history of education. Since the spread of compulsory schooling in the late nineteenth and early twentieth centuries, considerable rancor and debate have been focused on specific decisions about how America's children should be reared in public schools. Using schools as a means of reforming society by manipulating the consciousness of children has been an everyday part of the politics of American life for longer than any reader of this book can remember.

The official formulation of truth, proper behavior, and acceptable belief in the schools has never attained a coherence sufficient to prove the existence of a conspiracy to mold children to a single image. But the pressure of majority-approved socialization has so seriously restricted the ability of some families to preserve or develop unorthodox values and unpopular beliefs, that it is fair to refer to the prevailing school practices of any era as a form of publicly sponsored orthodoxy. This is true as far back as Horace Mann's efforts to make Christianity the basis of public-school reform and as recently as the debates over Darwinism and creationism in high-school science texts.

The history of conflict over school orthodoxy changed profoundly with the advent of compulsory attendance laws. Once the audience became virtually captive and the control became majoritarian, it was necessary for a variety of social groups to contest with each other over whose values and world view would be adopted by the local public school. Parents began to be viewed by educators as presumptively incompetent; and schooling became less an issue of individual development and family aspiration and more an issue of social needs and group values. Dissent became less and less legitimate while dissension became more and more inevitable.

As the majoritarian assumption took hold, public-education policy was transformed into a battleground for determining orthodoxy in a heterogeneous culture. Immigrant and ethnic groups, religious organizations, social reformers, jingoists, class interests all sought to have their own values legitimized and sustained by the schools. Although each has seen in schooling the triumph of different interests, the common insight of such diverse historians as Spring, Tyack, Katz, Nasaw, Bowles and Gintis is that schooling has essentially been a tool for the socialization of children. All agree that many of the struggles over schooling have been attempts to gain control of the socialization process or the values it transmits.

Compelling Belief moves the focus from past to present and attempts to appraise the cultural meaning and effect of modern conflicts over schooling and world view.

CENSORSHIP: THE WAR
OVER ORTHODOXY

Part One consists of six chapters describing current school wars in which families, public officials, and citizen groups fight for control of public school culture. Chapter 1 tells the story of a virulent incident of censorship in Warsaw, Indiana, an extreme example of an almost common experience. In Chapters 2, 3, 4, and 5 the common themes of a large number of censorship problems are described—their national proliferation, their sources in cultural confusion, and their individual and political casualties. Chapter 6 presents the law's one-eyed perception of the war over orthodoxy and shows why traditional civil libertarians have been unable to use law to end censorship in the schools. Throughout Part One it is suggested that so long as the law requires that contests for control of school socialization be decided by political majorities, there will always be dissenters whose beliefs and world views have been banned from the schools in violation of the Constitution.

1

Book Burning in Warsaw

Warsaw, Indiana, is a staid, middle-class town where most Americans would feel at home—hardly a likely place for an outbreak of political hysteria. But in 1977 and 1978, Warsaw suffered a massive seizure of anti-intellectualism that nearly exhausted the good will and common sense of its residents and left the town shaking. By the time the crisis had passed, five books had been banned, three teachers had been fired, the student newspaper had been eliminated, nine literature courses had been cut from the curriculum, and local senior citizens had offered their "vote of thanks" to the censors with a parking-lot bonfire fed by gasoline and high-school texts.

Sitting among the flat fields of an agriculturally abundant northern Indiana county halfway between South Bend and Fort Wayne, Warsaw is as industrial as its people are industrious. Next to Christian fundamentalism, its predominant ideology is the work ethic; and in 1978 it had an unemployment rate of under 4 percent to show for its efforts. The country's largest manufacturer of orthopedic appliances, several foundries, a branch of the country's biggest printing firm, and a farm-implements producer provide many of the jobs for the town's 9,600 residents. In the last twenty years the growth of these and other corporations brought an influx of highly trained workers and professionals whose backgrounds are more urban and more urbane than those of long-time residents.

Several of the old-timers still remember that nearby Winona Lake was home—from 1910 to 1935—to the born-again ex-baseball player and evangelist Billy Sunday. Sunday and the Christian fundamentalists who grew up around him and Warsaw were not comfortable with the encroachment of modernism, cities, sin, and the flabby moral relativism they saw threatening family structure, and they meant to wipe them out however they could.

Sunday was proud to say that he converted people to Christ at "less than two dollars per soul." His success as an evangelist can be measured by the fact that by 1920 he was worth over $1.5 million and by the diamond studs and patent-leather shoes he sported as he called people to "come down the sawdust trail" and give themselves to Christ. The success of Warsaw can be measured by the fact that it has a thriving economy, more than a handful of multimillionaires, and only a few pockets of poverty.

For all its big business and big religion, however, Warsaw is a small town. One local executive described it as a place where "you know whose check is good and whose husband is not." It is a town of thirty-six churches and one bookstore. In that bookstore there is an abundant collection of pornographic magazines, but you cannot buy a copy of the *New Republic* because the demand is insufficient. The people of Warsaw do not have to lock their doors and do not fear to walk the streets at night, but they report that they are suffering from pervasive boredom. One lifelong resident, who thinks the flatness of life is even more depressing to newcomers, observed that the censorship conflict created "something to do."

Prior to 1977 Warsaw had a school system that had responded very much like others in the country to the liberalizing trend in the educational philosophy that grew out of the sixties. The school board let the superintendent run the schools without much interference or questioning. The school system, in turn, built up a modest diversity of literature electives at the high school, offered a values clarification course to older students, and set up a voluntary Individually Guided Education program in one of its nine elementary schools. In 1974 collective bargaining was legislatively granted to teachers in Indiana.

Then, shortly before spring of 1977, the membership of the appointed school board became more conservative and more assertive about its power over the schools. On July 19, 1977, the board banned the textbook *Values Clarification,* which had been in use in an elective high-school course for two years. After a few minutes of reading selected exercises from the book, in which students are asked how they feel about topics such as divorce, marijuana, and premarital sex, the board passed a motion that called for the book to be "thrown out, removed, banned, destroyed, and forbidden to be used." The action was taken in direct violation of written policy requiring a review committee and a superintendent's recommendation for removal of library or instructional materials. Two months later the city's only newspaper, the *Times-Union,* reported that the Warsaw Senior Citizens Club planned to obtain the banned *Values Clarification* texts and burn them.

On August 25, 1977, the school board, again without following its own procedures, unanimously ordered the discontinuation of elective high-school courses, including Black Literature, Gothic Literature, Science Fiction, Folklore and Legends, and Whatever Happened to Mankind? The action effectively eliminated the elective literature program and replaced it with vocabulary, grammar, and composition courses.

As the fall term began at Warsaw High School, principal Smith called Teresa Burnau, an English teacher who had been assigned a Women in Literature course, to his office to discuss books she had ordered for her class. Smith forbade her to use *The Stepford Wives* and *Growing Up Female in America*, because "someone in the community might be offended" by their criticism of traditional roles for women.

Then, in mid-October, the principal struck again, this time summoning Ms. Burnau to his office and ordering her to discontinue using *Go Ask Alice,* the anonymous and depressing diary of a teenage girl whose involvement with drugs leads to her death. Smith banned the book because it contained obscenities. The elimination of *Go Ask Alice* was followed by a directive to all teachers to bring to the principal "any materials you have in your room that might be objectionable."

Another English teacher, Arleen Miner, then brought in *Student Critic,* which had been in use for three years. It contained the words "hell" and "damn." Ms. Miner, unable to ink the words out, cut the offending pages from the books before returning them to her literary-criticism students.

As the school term moved toward Thanksgiving, Ms. Burnau found she was not permitted to use *The Bell Jar* by Sylvia Plath. Although Ms. Burnau offered to secure permission slips from parents for use of the book and to assign a different book for those who found *The Bell Jar* objectionable, the book continued to be banned.

On December 15, the Senior Citizens Club made good on its promise and burned forty copies of *Values Clarification* in a parking-lot ceremony. The president of the 200-member group defended himself against charges of evoking images of nazism by claiming that he was only carrying out his obligation to the club. Perhaps it was this action that encouraged one board member to quip, in defense of a ban on "objectionable materials," that teachers will "have no problem knowing the will of this community."

Having removed the offensive books, the board moved on to the teachers. On April 17, 1978, three teachers, including Teresa Burnau and Joann Dupont, secretary of the Warsaw Teachers' Union and outspoken critic of the board's policies, were notified that their contracts would not be renewed. No substantial criticism of teaching performance was made concerning the fired teachers.

After the teachers came the students. In late May a student editorial criticizing the firing of Ms. Burnau and Ms. Dupont was published after the principal reversed an earlier refusal to allow it to be printed. The student newspaper was subsequently shut down, but students were allowed to submit articles to the *Times-Union* for publication. The owner of the *Times-Union*, Reub Williams, is a powerful figure in town, and he had strongly influenced the appointment of the four new school-board members who were pursuing censorship most vigorously.

Just when it seemed the door had been shut on smut, Carl Davis, a concerned member of the community, read selections from *Go Ask Alice* at a board meeting even though the book was no longer in use. The excerpts, consisting of profanity and other street language, were printed verbatim by the *Times-Union*. For the next two weeks editorials and letters condemning filthy language in school texts appeared regularly. On June 21 the paper ran a front-page story announcing the formation of People Who Care, an organization dedicated to removing "filthy, vulgar material from the classroom." The next day an ad paid for by an anonymous donor soliciting support for People Who Care appeared, claiming that Warsaw teachers favored vulgar material in class.

The purpose of all this activity became clearer several days later when the Indiana Education Employment Relations Board began four days of hearings on charges of unfair labor practices brought by the Warsaw Teachers' Union. The union had claimed that the unilateral elimination of books and courses violated the state's labor law. An enormous number of townspeople attended the hearings and attempted to make them into a forum for discussing obscenity. The hearing examiner, Robert Lingenfelter, characterized the meeting, the longest in the state's history, as a "parallel to the Scopes Monkey Trial" of 1925 in which William Jennings Bryan and Clarence Darrow fought the battle of

Genesis versus Darwinism in the Tennessee town of Dayton. Lingenfelter credited the *Times-Union* with whipping up an hysterical atmosphere that led, in his view, to "the obstruction of justice" by townspeople.

In an editorial appearing a week after the hearing, the *Times-Union* executive editor, William Mollenhour, fed the obstructionist tendency by revealing that "allied forces" had seized a copy of "Communist Rules for Revolution" in Dusseldorf in 1919 and that "fifty [sic] years later the Reds are still following them." At the top of the list of rules was "Corrupt the young; get them away from religion, get them interested in sex. Make them superficial; destroy their ruggedness." After the hearings, political pressures were brought to bear on the governor and other state officials to get them to intervene in the legal process and influence Lingenfelter's decision.

Some residents of Warsaw claim that the conflict over the control of students' minds lay dormant during the winter, like the fertile fields of wheat and soybeans that surround the town. But in early spring of 1979, four suits were filed in federal district court in Indiana challenging the censorship. One of the suits, *Zykan* v. *Warsaw Community School Corporation*, was brought by a seventeen-year-old high-school student on behalf of herself and other like-minded students. Brooke Zykan challenged the school board's actions in "prohibiting teachers from using certain books and ordering the removal of certain courses." The class-action suit asked for a restoration of books and courses and the requirement that a fair and reasonable process be used by the board in any future censorship decisions.

The basis of the suit was the First Amendment right of free inquiry and the right of academic freedom and open expression. According to Joseph Bauer, a professor of law at nearby Notre Dame, who was the Civil Liberties Union lawyer representing the students, the central question in the suit was "whether a school board has a right to remove books and courses and fire teachers because they are inconsistent with the board's social and political values."

8

The claim that the U.S. Constitution applies in Warsaw generated the early signs of the same hysteria that built up over the presence of dirty words in books and the appearance of labor arbitrators in Warsaw in 1978. At least one family involved in the suit received two anonymous, obscene letters addressed "Dear smut peddlers" and inviting them to get out of town and "take your smutty family and your rotten concepts along with you."

Although People Who Care found the antismut angle to be a successful headline grabber and a useful tool in winning battles in Warsaw, the members and their supporters, estimated at between four hundred and eighteen hundred, were not primarily concerned about obscenity. Like Billy Sunday, who gave up professional baseball, drinking, swearing, and gambling for the scriptural faith of fundamentalism, many of these people felt their traditional family values were threatened and at risk of decay. And, like Billy Sunday, they are as articulate as they are vehement about the preservation and extension of their views.

At an informal meeting of People Who Care, one man, a mechanical engineer, preached the group's view using Solzhenitsyn's Harvard commencement speech on the spiritual exhaustion of the West as his text. "The issue of censorship and propriety of books," the concerned citizen said, is "but one brush fire, which is part of a potential prairie fire seeking to engulf the United States and the world." The rise of women's liberation and schools that will not support fundamentalist values of authority and family hierarchy must share the blame for this prairie fire. As appreciative antifeminist comments circulated around the room, it became clear why Teresa Burnau and the books in the Women in Literature course had been banned in Warsaw.

Conversations with numerous Warsaw residents indicate that authority is a central issue in these people's lives—authority of men over women, of fundamentalism over secular humanism, of the school board over the teachers, of the family over the school board, and of parents over children. At bottom, these people sensed that their value system was

9

seriously threatened, and some Warsaw parents were willing to tolerate censorship, obstruction of the legal process, and destruction of teaching careers to preserve their ideas. The excesses to which apparently well-meaning people in Warsaw had been led—scripted by the local media and played out in school-board shouting matches and circuslike hearings, and through old-fashioned intimidation—created a climate of fear that chilled the exercise of freedoms of speech, press, and inquiry and effectively suspended the First Amendment in Warsaw.

There were, in fact, many parents in Warsaw who opposed the actions of the school board and looked to the federal district court to overturn them. But these dissenting parents felt they could not afford to speak out. One woman said she would have liked to have supported the high-school students' suit but that if she had, her husband's business would have been ruined. The religious faction, she said, "seems to have great power over what is done and said." A professional who hoped for some sort of compromise pointed out that "obviously there's a lot of power being wielded here, and your career can be ruined if you talk about it." What most people were afraid to talk about was that much of this power was being wielded by the owner of the newspaper.

If fear neutralized community support for the plaintiffs and for freedom of speech, it cast a pall on the high-school faculty and converted academic freedom into bureaucratic order. As a result of the campaign of censorship, one English teacher saw a growth of self-imposed censorship and paranoia among teachers. Not only was there fear; there was fear of discussing fear.

High-school students in Warsaw are the people who have suffered most from the restrictions placed on teachers, schoolbooks, and curriculum. The dozen students I spoke with described the change in their high school during the past two years as an experience of being "dragged down" intellectually and being personally bullied and intimidated

10

when taking any action to change things. Although they freely acknowledged that some students support the school board, they claimed "there are many more on our side than anybody really thinks." Intercoms were described as two-way listening devices for administrative surveillance of teachers and students; continuing censorship of yearbook production and of reading materials was alleged; and personal searches and locker searches by police dogs were related. In one lively discussion of the school, all the students agreed that it was "as bad as *The Scarlet Letter.*"

For all their spirited resentment at having their education become the pawn of a local social struggle, these students went out of their way to show that they did not disrespect their parents, even though they differed strongly with some of their fundamentalist views. Many had read at least one of the banned books and did not see what all the fuss was about. But they felt they could not be any more public or energetic about their own interests. One eighteen-year-old seemed to see how she too might become a fearful parent and support intimidation and condone hysteria: "If you don't go to college and you stay here for a year, Warsaw will get its claws in you, and you'll never leave."

The then school superintendent, Dr. Charles Bragg, was also swept along by the fear of public accusation and by the polarizing irrationality of conflict over orthodoxy. As he focused on the competing values of those who struggle to have themselves declared the majority that rules the schools, he became uncomfortable and confused: "I am a traditional person. I am a progressive. I just want the education that is best for the kids." The hysteria in town had removed the possibility of diversity or compromise, and Bragg knew that his own survival depended on knowing who speaks for the majority in Warsaw.

The hysteria over smut in Warsaw's schools became a cover beneath which personal and political agendas were carried out, political bases were created or destroyed, and insecurities about modern life were vented. Warsaw is an antiunion town in which the teachers' union is new and disliked by management. The obscenity-in-schools struggle had been used to weaken the teachers' union, split it, and cover up the arbitrary firing of teachers. One local politician, who campaigned to create an elective school board, pinpointed this aspect of the power struggle in an ad that read: "The current thinly disguised union-busting activities promoted by the local media monopoly have ruined the careers of several very capable teachers while forcing others out of the community."

Beneath all this, it was politics as usual in Warsaw. The town had been run for years, according to several insistently anonymous residents, by one man, the owner of the local radio station and newspaper. By orchestrating a combination of school-board appointments and an antismut media blitz, and by keeping citizens' groups unaware of whose interests they really served, he extended his sphere of influence to include the schools—while People Who Care was given the feeling that *they* had won some influence over children's education.

Asked what a school board should do when confronted with two groups of parents whose values and beliefs were diametrically opposed, one member of People Who Care answered in a single breath: "Let the majority rule. No problem. School decisions should be based on the absolutes of Christian behavior." He could not see himself in the minority, as fundamentalists in most parts of America are. This assumption that schooling decisions are the province of the majority made possible, perhaps even inevitable, the hysteria in Warsaw and in the increasing number of other places wracked by censorship struggles.

Zykan v. *Warsaw* was dismissed in 1979 by a federal district court for failure to state a constitutional claim. On appeal to the federal circuit court in 1980, the way was opened for a trial to show that the Warsaw school board had acted to impose an antifeminist orthodoxy on the plaintiff high-school students. But by that time the Zykan family had left town, resources and witnesses were scarce, and the civil liberties attorney consented to a dismissal of the case. Teacher Teresa Burnau had also left town having accepted a Washington secretarial job and a trifling settlement for her dismissal from the Warsaw school system. A new majority had established an old orthodoxy in the schools, at least until a competing group of parents and politicians organize themselves to impose yet another set of beliefs upon schoolteachers and children.

2
Parents versus Parents:
PAST AND PRESENT

> Probably no deeper division of our people can proceed from
> any provocation than from finding it necessary to choose what
> doctrine and whose program public education officials shall
> compel youth to unite in embracing.
>
> —Justice Jackson, *West Virginia* v. *Barnette* (1943)

Warsaw is not unique. The level of conflict over books in
America's public schools has been increasing dramatically.
Studies by groups as diverse as the Association of American Publishers and the National Council of Teachers of English have estimated that up to 30 percent of the nation's
school districts have experienced book and curriculum conflicts in the past few years and that these battles are becoming more widespread. The results of these often heated
disputes include tenseness and distrust among parents,
teachers, and school officials; the polarization of communities; and the breakdown of the process of school governance. Reports in the public media suggest that no community, no belief, and no author is immune to the growing

effort to control the ideology of public schools through control of their libraries and curriculums.

In Indiana books were burned because they raised questions about divorce, drug abuse, and premarital sex; and an English teacher was fired because she did not hold traditional views on the role of women in society. Elsewhere it is the same. Solzhenitsyn is banned in Maine as well as Moscow; Malamud is viewed as anti-Semitic in Levittown, New York, and is trashed along with Langston Hughes who is alleged by white school board members to be "anti-Negro"; Maurice Sendak's four-year-old character Mickey must wear Magic Marker shorts in *In the Night Kitchen* lest the kindergartners of Springfield, Missouri, be corrupted. The texts of Oregon must not cast aspersions on the Founding Fathers, and those of Louisiana must teach the benefits of free-enterprise economics. Sex-role stereotypes must be removed from books in Montgomery County, Maryland; the junior-high-school children in one district of New York City may not read about life in Spanish Harlem; books are screened for racial stereotypes and Huck Finn is finished in Winnetka, Illinois. The legislature of Arkansas insists that Genesis be given equal time with evolution; whole dictionaries are banned because they contain multiple definitions for "bed," "knock," and "shack."

In the explicit curriculums of public schools, socialism, materialism, secular humanism, elitism, individualism, escapism, ageism, women's liberation, Darwinism, religion, sexism, permissiveness, conformism, and just about anything capable of being labeled has been attacked. From ideological, political, and religious crusaders to racial, moral, and sexual objectors, the number of people fighting with each other over what the schools should, or should not, teach has increased dramatically in the last five years.

The American Library Association, which monitors these developments with obvious horror, believes that censorship is more vicious, more sophisticated, and more widespread than it has been at any time since the days of Joseph McCarthy and reports a quantum leap in book challenges following

15

the election of 1980. Scores of state and national organizations of all political stripe, but generally reflecting the rightward swing of American politics, have sprung up to aid and encourage the censors. Where Americans inflicted with McCarthyism suspected that aliens lurked under every bed, it is between the covers of every book that the search for unacceptable ideas is conducted today.

While the phenomenon may seem a simple confrontation between good and evil to the casual observer on either side, censorship is in fact a highly complex set of reactions to the faulty design of America's school systems. Beneath the surface of what is often described as the struggle of the narrow-minded against the open-minded, families are taking seriously the 100-year-old ideology of compulsory schooling: that to be concerned with the education of one's own children is human but to be concerned with the education of everyone else's children is divine. Censorship is more than just censorship. It is a battle over the transmission of culture required by a system that prescribes majority control of education decisions for all but the wealthy. The conflict often threatens to go out of control because it reflects a cultural crisis in which our common assumptions seem less and less able either to explain the present or to give guidance for the future. To evaluate censorship and describe its consequences for politics and personal conscience, we must begin with some reflections on what most Americans have believed about public schooling.

The health of American public education depends almost entirely upon the existence of a rough consensus of values among families on a local basis. How Americans understand the past, behave in the present, and predict the future are all assumed to be reflected in the experiences children have in school. This ideology of schooling holds not only that our most local political institution should reflect the existing consensus of values but that it should be a social instrument for the reform of those values and the perfection of national and personal character. When the public begins to believe that the consensus is weakening, a battle for the control of socialization in the schools becomes necessary.

The emotions that are engaged by the battle for control of socialization in schools are one indication that these conflicts cut to the personal and cultural core, touching beliefs, faith, conscience, and the assumptions that inform the relationship between generations. But these emotions also cloud the public issues at stake, drawing the participants and the observers alike into a narrowly focused sense of urgency about their self-interest.

Although the combatants often seem to take themselves too seriously, it would be a mistake to slight these deeply felt concerns of sincere and troubled parents or to make light of the substantial damage these conflicts have caused all the participants. In fact there are books, rules of behavior, curriculums, and even teachers offensive to many who take the time to examine how their children are being educated. It seems that parents can usually find some fundamental value difference between their family and the least common denominator in the public school. Racial and gender stereotypes abound. History texts and history itself are made and remade to suit the dominant ethic of the times. Religion and morality are not taken seriously. Dysfunctional values are taught, and young minds are bureaucratized.

There are always issues of conscience in school curriculums and texts. Because teaching can never avoid giving shape and form to the world through the assumption of attitudes, the selection of facts, and the dependence on some faith, no matter how mundane, the schools can never be value-neutral. Competing groups of parents, though they may sometimes be used by larger political interests, cannot be faulted for feeling that their own understandings of life are threatened in the world at large or for trying to find a way to prevent their children from inheriting the alienation of adults in the community through the schools.

The censorship of schoolbooks and the struggle for control of texts and curriculum are not new; but prior to the

17

entrenchment of universal compulsory schooling in the last part of the nineteenth century, many of the value conflicts that might have been played out as contests over texts and curriculum took a very different form. The number of escape valves available to families that disagreed with public-school policy was greater not only in the absence of legal compulsion to attend but in the parental power to determine parts of a child's curriculum in public school.

A series of court cases traces the emergence of the tip of the censorship iceberg and shows, with a few exceptions, the deference of the courts and Constitution to the political process on these issues. The earliest widespread conflict over texts and teaching came with the rise of fundamentalism and nationalism in the twenties. In one landmark case the state of Nebraska had legislated an end to all foreign-language instruction in public and private schools, a xenophobic act directed primarily at German-language instruction in private schools. The Supreme Court, in 1923, declared unconstitutional such close restriction on what may be taught. But this case, even when combined two years later with the famous *Pierce* ruling that families may not be compelled constitutionally to attend public schools only, left an enormous and vague area in which it was unknown to what extent the political process could be used to prescribe the values children must be taught.

As the twenties wore on, the efforts of the increasingly powerful fundamentalist sects were directed at preventing the teaching of evolution and at resurrecting the conflict of Genesis and Darwinism, which had stayed below the surface of public life since the third quarter of the nineteenth century. The Genesis textbook crusaders were not stopped by the legal defense in the Scopes trial or by the steamy spectacle of William Jennings Bryan jousting with Clarence Darrow in Dayton, Tennessee, that year.

Scopes was convicted, and in the ensuing decade anti-evolution bills were introduced in thirty-seven states. The attempt to control this aspect of textbooks was so successful that for nearly thirty years biology texts made almost no serious mention of Darwinism and the theory of evolution. To this day the average high-school biology text contains fewer than fifty lines about evolution. It was not until 1968 that the Supreme Court invalidated a state law prohibiting evolutionist texts and teachings on the ground that such activity constituted an establishment of religion in the public schools.

In 1943 the Supreme Court handed down *West Virginia* v. *Barnette,* a ruling with a startlingly clear recognition that using the public schools to manipulate the beliefs of students posed substantial dangers to liberty and to the governance process in the school systems. The Court struck down the use of the pledge of allegiance and flag salute in public-school classrooms as an invasion of the "sphere of intellect and spirit" of students. The First Amendment ruling was explicitly not based upon the religious scruples of the plaintiffs; yet it recognized that in ideology, as in religious belief, government coercion breeds irreconcilable conflict over orthodoxy: "As governmental pressure toward unity becomes greater, so strife becomes more bitter as to whose unity it shall be." Even the right to attend an alternative to public school as declared in *Pierce* did not convince the Court that struggles over curriculum and teaching in public schools were acceptable from a First Amendment point of view. The shock of recognition in *Barnette* did not last, and the principles it enunciated have remained underutilized and often unexplored.

The fifties saw another wave of censorship, this one accompanying the anxiety and intolerance of McCarthyism and hysterial anticommunism. As Mary Raywid's detailed study, *The Axe-Grinders,* shows, the censors were an interlocking directorate of political rightists who found support among ordinary people whose values were not those of the mainstream. During this time the Supreme Court handled a number of cases involving teacher loyalty oaths and laws prohibiting the teaching of "subversive" ideas. While many of the laws were struck down, the Court's actions covered a range of technical issues. The question of academic freedom was only rarely discussed, and the Court completely avoided the problem of a conflict between a majoritarian institution for compulsory socialization of children and individual freedom of belief. That the schools had become a battleground for competing ideologies was formally unrecognized.

Even in the religious cases of the early sixties, schooling was not perceived as a socializing institution. The Court was willing to declare that the wall of separation of church and state prevented the introduction of religious ceremony in the public schools. But it did not recognize the existence of *secular* indoctrination in schools, and it failed to notice that religion was but one of many motivations for community conflict over schooling and socialization. Had it done so, it would have given powerful impetus to those interested in contesting texts and curriculums then in use.

None of these censorship themes—religion, science, or jingoism—has disappeared. They can all be found imbedded in the more varied modern censorship controversies to which antifeminism has been added as a major theme. Two things appear to be shared by the older and the newer struggles over values in text and curriculum: The intense emotion and widespread polarization they generate, and the persistent refusal of courts to examine the possibility that the war over orthodoxy in schools is the modern equivalent of the war over state religions fought in the seventeenth and eighteenth centuries.

The history of text and curriculum contests and schooling in general may be viewed as a process in which the public makes demands of the school system as a socializing institution at those times when society experiences deep value conflict or uncertainty. The schools are then expected to become the remedial source of social cohesion.

3

Culture on the Brink:

HEATING UP THE WAR
OVER ORTHODOXY

When the way is lost then come the laws.
—Lao Tse

Censorship of schoolbooks and teaching is, among other things, an attempt to impose meaning on social order and, in the process, to define personal identity. The myriad of petty struggles to condone or condemn books used in classroom and library are reactions to the alienating confusion of a culture in which customary explanations no longer seem to have the power to explain very much. Two broad categories of these efforts to enlist government power behind private ideology can be identified from an examination of the hundreds of incidents of censorship across the country: ideologically articulate censorship and scapegoating censorship. By very different means each type tries to cope with what the censors feel is the culture-wide collapse of explanations. The term "censorship" is used to include all kinds of struggles over books and curriculums whether involving removal or initial selection.

Scapegoating

In the largest number of censorship incidents (according to a National Council of Teachers of English survey), those protesting curriculum or the content of books in school libraries have no discernable point of view. They are simply *against* whatever books they choose to be against. Antagonism and exclusion are more important to them than content. Their declared reasons—the means by which they elicit the support of other citizens and eventually of the school board—are often that the books contain "filth," "obscenity," "vulgar language," or "smut." The words and phrases offered to demonstrate these contentions are taken out of context and used without regard to the overall intent, tone, or significance of the book. It is almost never claimed that the books are obscene in the legal sense—that is, that they are sexually explicit appeals to prurient interests and devoid of redeeming social value. These books are simply "dirty" and must be banned.

The outcry against smut is no more than a politically useful tool that enables parents and other community members to have the joint experience of successfully exercising power over schools by banning something, anything. Because there are in fact few shared values among the participants, an attack on a book can generate more emotion than can be created by supporting a book's replacement.

One technique for generating political power without advancing any point of view other than nihilism involves doublespeak. The action of the Island Trees School Board in New York is an example of making reasoned discussion impossible. On the advice of a state-wide schoolbook sanitizing group called PONY-U (now defunct), the school board removed several novels from the high-school library including Bernard Malamud's *The Fixer*. The school board appointed a committee of teachers and community members to present information about the offensiveness of the books after the banning decision. On the committee was a man who, when asked what he saw in Malamud's novel that was "anti-Semitic," replied that he did not have to answer, that he had "a vote like everyone else on the committee," and that he was "voting to ban *The Fixer* because it was anti-Semitic." The same "reasoning" convicted Langston Hughes of being "anti-Negro."

These techniques provoke the involvement of people who are immune to reason as well as those who believe that once the claim of impurity is raised, reasoning ends. The polarization of neighbors that is created by these techniques is a sad spectacle, for it is instigated by people who are sensitive to the breakdown of social cohesion and long for its recreation. Those who begin with a sense of alienation end by gaining a transient feeling that they have an identity because they can at least define who they are not. A situation that is perceived as being confused, chaotic, or anarchic becomes momentarily understandable. The ambiguous, complex, and unsettling visions of literature and of life are defined as evil.

The polarity of thought is matched by the polarization of community. Because other members of the community resist the efforts of the censors, the struggle can be extended over time; and the experience of projecting evil outside the group can be repeated and reinforced. On a primitive level, which few will acknowledge in the heat of conflict, people who sense the breakdown of shared community values are able to create the illusion that there are in fact still some values that hold the community together. It is, of course, an unconsciously self-destructive means of creating community, like labeling women as witches and burning them at the stake. But this method of censorship is as old as the witch hunt and as modern as McCarthyism. All three—censorship, the witch hunt, and McCarthyism—create and exploit the political hysteria that is symptomatic of a partial breakdown of cultural values and assumptions. All three are aimed at creating, at any cost, social cohesion, and all three are open to easy exploitation by individuals and groups seeking power in the name of the common good. Scapegoating censorship feeds on alienation and transforms it into hostility.

Ideology in the Forefront

Sometimes censorship is ideologically articulate and purposeful, leaving room for opposing groups of parents to fight in the open over what doctrines schools should adhere to. Such censorship begins with an attempt to kill off a "false" vision so that it can be replaced by a "true" vision. Literature, which can be a source of vision about the future as well as a statement of the reality of the present, is often the object of this censorship. One example among many is the use of government power in Warsaw, Indiana, to eliminate books dealing with the oppression of women in society. The action of the censors on this subject was a reaction of traditional values against the threat of modernism. The town was awash in the vaguely understood and unsettling possibility that the beliefs of the parents would not be adopted by the children and that parental attitudes might fail to control the future. Hundreds of men and women discovered a sense of community and were articulate about woman's place in the hierarchy of God as they sought to sweep out *The Bell Jar* and *The Stepford Wives*. As one man put it, "Children seek the parent to restrain them. A woman inherently seeks for man to be in authority over her, and man seeks God to be in authority over him. It is not a question of equality . . . it is a question of a required condition for stable society."

A spokesperson for People Who Care received the nodding approval of her fellow members when she claimed that they had nothing against the Warsaw high-school course on "women in literature." They only wished that if the teacher had to discuss women, she would discuss women that young girls could look up to, like Jane Eyre. Issues of feminism and authority closely intertwined with their view that the schools must be the servant of the parents and must not contradict parental values. Clearly, the majority of parents in Warsaw felt that the "absolutes of Christian morality" should be reflected in all their children saw and heard in the publicly owned and operated schools.

But the town harbored an equally articulate, less politically powerful group of parents whose experiences told them
that women's roles were changing, that the long history of
gender was indeed oppressive, and that authoritarianism
was a false god. For these more "liberal" parents the status
quo school values were adequate. That literature should reflect the change and uncertainty and injustice of life was as it
should be for "liberal" parents. The battle over books and
teaching eventually moved to state and federal legal proceedings in which each of the competing groups wanted to
show that their values and world view should become the
official reality ordained by law. It is hard to know which
group should be called "censors" in such a school war, except if one assumes that censorship is the work of people out
of power trying to take control from people in power. In
Warsaw censorship coincided with a conservative takeover
of the school board and pointed out to a community only
dimly aware of them, the value choices made by schools in
the ordinary process of policy making.

Both sides sought to control value orthodoxy by controlling literature and curriculum. But where the minority
sought the right to have the children read Plath and the
others if their parents so desired, the fundamentalists sought
to ban such visions from the school altogether. Their insistence on the rightness of their way was a reflection of the
confusion beneath their certainty and the threat they perceived to their vision of life. Their longing for the customary
and organic cohesion of the social network became a demand
for order, however mechanical, however imposed. Their
claim to parental rights for the majority became an act of
repression against the minority.

Ironically, the liberal opponents of this censorship could
cloak their desire to maintain control of school values in the
honorific phrases of freedom of expression. Each side feared
a society dominated by the other's values and wanted to
protect their children from the false visions of the others'
beliefs. But those whose values had already been established

25

tried to defend them with the claim that majority control of curriculum amounted to censorship. Clearly, it was censorship; but what they failed to mention was that the process by which any books or curriculums are selected—even by liberals—is also censorship. Whoever wins a battle for control of orthodoxy in schools is, by definition, a censor.

Like scapegoating censorship, this more ideologically articulate battle for control of culture transmission proceeds from the vague realization that the culture no longer holds the power of explanation. The scapegoater's reaction to cultural weightlessness has been to define self and culture negatively—to create the feeling of social morality by externalizing an illusion of educational immorality. The ideological book battlers react to the collapse of cultural explanations by attempting to impose their own, usually conservative, explanation and world view on school curriculum. To them, culture can be legislated by school boards. For both kinds of censors, issues as deeply personal and fundamentally nonrational as gender roles, authoritarianism, the meaning of life, and the shape of consciousness must be fought out through political mechanisms as mundane as school-board elections.

Whatever process of compromise of values might arise from policy making in schools has been rendered useless by the politics of intolerance and polarization. If the lack of social cohesion gives rise to censorship, the emotional tactics of the censors make the creation of cohesion more unlikely than ever. But the parents who initiate or are drawn into the battle over orthodoxy in the schools cannot be justly condemned for their concern over the future of children or culture. However much they may have transformed their private insecurity into moral rectitude or their affection for their children into inflammatory attacks on their neighbors, these parents are reacting to a common dilemma. To offer a wholesale condemnation of those who are struggling to be free of cultural confusion is to indict oneself.

The claim that community values must be rejuvenated through social institutions is an angry and fearful expression of those who feel that society is losing its harmony as the dissonance between experience and ideology increases. For example, most of us absorbed almost unconsciously from childhood the assumption that if each of us pursued his or her own well-being individually, the net result would be justly labeled "the common good." By this calculus, individualism and "looking out for number one" were not selfish but were expressions of human dignity and independence. Yet every day's experience with inflation and unemployment offers proof that we require a collective response that is beyond the reach of our assumptions about self and life—that the common sense Einstein called "that layer of bias laid down in the mind before age eighteen" has become an education against survival. It is not our politicians but our culture that has been lying to us. To see a problem like inflation as one requiring a collective solution would require us to dismantle a basic part of our understanding of culture and personality. Our daily experience, then, suggests that the individualist ideology does not work as it once did. When enough of these ideological assumptions become inoperative, a crisis of explanations looms, and censorship, though not defensible, becomes predictable.

If we cannot generate an empathy for the alienation expressed by censors, then perhaps another approach to understanding their actions will suffice. School censors, and those who do battle with them, do nothing more than what the common ideology of schooling has taught them to do. They take seriously the message embedded in one hundred years of compulsory, universal, publicly funded schooling: that public education is the great cohesive force of a democratic society, capable of being used to continuously improve personal consciousness and national character.

In the wake of the moralism of Horace Mann, American culture has supported and strengthened the idea that the battle for men's souls can be fought through compulsory education. The censors do nothing fundamentally different from what is done by the "selectors" of books or designers of curriculum, who are elected to state and local school boards, trained in schools of education, or elected to legislatures.

27

The censors have simply learned what the nation's schools have taught by their structure and action: that there is more at stake in influencing the education of other children than in controlling the education of your own.

On a still more mundane level, conversations with dozens of parents involved in battles over books and teachers make it clear that these people are seeking to redress an imbalance of power over their children's education. The growth of professional control of school administration and the eclipse of meaningful relationships between parents and teachers have left families with the feeling that they have lost custody of the child who goes to school. Parents who want their values and concerns for their children expressed in schooling are increasingly met with a wall of professional hostility and bureaucratic lethargy. It is not surprising that these people, unable as they are to procure private instruction, should turn to an organized battle to regain control of the schools. Political action is a reasonable answer to the lack of responsiveness of schools to the endlessly varied needs and aspirations of families. As censorship battles begin to show parents that there must always be losers as well as winners in the battle over values in school, the reasonable response becomes the only available response. The desire for more family power over a child's education is transformed by the zero-sum game of school policy into a political war over public orthodoxy.

4

Resurrection of Theocracy:

THE SPECIAL CASE OF CREATIONISM

The war over public orthodoxy takes the form not only of exclusion of unwanted books and ideas from public schools but of the forced inclusion of ideologies competing with the dominant ethic in the schools. One such situation is the spreading legal and political campaign of the so-called scientific creationists. Unlike the supporters of the law that led to the infamous but endlessly entertaining Scopes trial, these ideological warriors do not seek to make the teaching of Darwinism a crime but seek to get Genesis into the nation's approved biology textbooks. The lesson of the modern struggle between God and science, which is beginning to be played out on the field of public-school policy making, lies in the range of differences between the two sides. It is a battle over the epistemology of daily life.

Scientific creationism has been making itself felt most sharply in state-wide processes for the selection (not the censorship) of public-school textbooks. In addition to mounting political campaigns in the twenty-two states that have state-wide textbook adoption procedures, the scientific creationists have supported legislation in at least fifteen states to require the teaching of Genesis alongside evolution. The effort is not restricted to the nation's Bible Belt but has been at least partially successful in states as geographically and socially disparate as Minnesota, California, Texas, Arkansas, and New York.

The tenor of the creationist/evolutionist controversies has ranged from the staid arguments of scientists over the evidence supporting each concept to the sometimes demagogic claims of true believers. The Honorable Braswell Deen, Jr., chief justice of the Georgia Court of Appeals, not long ago, ". . . made the case that the religious philosophy that now dominates our government and educational systems is atheistic humanistic evolution . . . [which] has conditioned our people for pro-abortion, infanticide, euthanasia, and cancerous crimes of all types." The judge's claims were made in a report to the state judiciary on the causes of crime.

In another corner of the country Nell Segraves, who has been laboring for her vision of Christian belief since the early sixties, has recently written that "it was easy to show that evolution is a principle of naturalism, which is basic to atheistic, agnostic, irreligious teachings and is the foundation of Communistic, Socialistic philosophy."

Those who have defended evolution and Darwinism from the creationist attack have also lapsed into demagoguery and defensive ridicule at times. Scientists supporting the idea that there is in fact evidence for creation as well as evolution have been attacked by critics as "false authorities" who "get their doctorates in a box of Cracker-Jacks" and as a "bunch of right-wing conservatives . . . [who] indulge in every kind of logical fallacy to state a rather over-blown case." Alongside this hyperbolic rhetoric of charge and countercharge, a deadly serious battle has been going on.

The conflict is not unlike current battles to get prayer back into the schools or to provide public funds for sectarian education. All attempt to enlist the power of government behind the expression of religious values in the schools. The scientific creationists are more sophisticated than the fundamentalists of an earlier era whose campaign to ban evolution altogether ended in a 1968 Supreme Court ruling that such a ban amounted to an establishment of fundamentalist religious beliefs. In one way, all these efforts to inject theology into schooling are noticeably similar to textbook battles based on secular values. Struggles over such things as the role of women in society, racial stereotypes, the structure of authority, and the values justifying economic systems may be nominally secular. But whether secular or religious, all these ideological interests are seeking control of the political apparatus of schooling. The Creation-Science Report of July 1979 recognizes this battle for control when, after noting that $5 million has been appropriated by Congress under the Elementary and Secondary Education Act (ESEA) for state citizenship education programs, it states that "until we can agree on whose values and ethics we are going to implement . . . *no values can be taught* by tax supported school personnel" (emphasis in original).

The tactics of the creationists are to make a claim for "equal time" for creationism with evolution and to try to demonstrate the equal scientific respectability of creationism through experts. In this way they are able to capture the traditional political claim for tolerance, pluralism, and free inquiry while avoiding charges that they seek to establish their religious beliefs in school texts. Such tactics mask the fact that many creationists sleep in the same political bed with intolerant and anti-intellectual elements of the right wing, which have opposed ERA, choice in childbearing, racial equality, and any form of dissent from Christian fundamentalist views of the world. In spite of this confusion of tactics and in spite of the political associations of its supporters, the creationist movement has succeeded in raising basic questions about the ideology established in American schools.

One vehicle for examining these questions was the California state court suit brought in 1978 by a broad class of citizens and taxpayers. The aim of the suit was to enjoin the state board of education from publishing and using a "science framework" that would have had the effect of making it impossible for local school districts to purchase biology textbooks containing discussions of creationism. The suit claimed that evolution is only a theory of the origin and development of life and that there are other valid theories on this subject, namely, scientific creationism. No mention is made of the validity of the creation theories of Hinduism, Buddhism, Shinto, or the Hopi Indians.

Much of the "evidence" offered for scientific creationism à la Genesis was actually a demonstration of the issues in the theory of evolution. Because evolution and scientific creationism were both alleged to be acceptable scientifically, it was urged that the state had no constitutional basis upon which to adopt one theory for its texts without discussing the other theory or to treat one as fact and the other as theory. It was denied that scientific creationism is a religion or religious doctrine.

The suit also claimed that "the theory of evolution cannot be proven beyond doubt and necessarily involves an element of faith." Quoting Professor Harrison Mathews, an evolutionist, the creationists' brief claims that:

> Belief in the theory of evolution is thus exactly parallel to belief in special creation—both are concepts which believers know to be true; but neither up to the present has been capable of proof.

It was argued that the faith required to accept evolution makes it a religion. The brief then linked evolution with "secular humanism," which was claimed to be a religion that may not be "established" in schools because of the First Amendment. Thus the court was asked to take its pick: either evolution is a religion and may not be included in the "science framework" without violating the Establishment Clause or both evolution and scientific creationism are scientifically valid theories that must get equal time in the state's approved biology textbooks. An attempt was made to reconcile these seemingly contradictory views of creationism and evolution by claiming that the requisite government neutrality toward religion can be satisfied by requiring equal time for the two theories, whether they be scientific or religious.

The creationists have attempted to capitalize more aggressively upon their intentional misunderstanding of science and academic freedom through their legislative campaign. In March of 1981 the Balanced Treatment for Creation-Science and Evolution-Science Act was signed into law by the governor of Arkansas, requiring that "balanced treatment" be given to "evolution-science and creation-science" in classroom lectures, textbook materials, library materials, and other educational programs in the public schools wherever "the subject of the origin of man, life, the earth, or the universe" are dealt with. The law further required that only "scientific evidences," and not religious instruction, be given as part of this balanced treatment. In December of 1981 a trial was held in federal district court in Little Rock on the claim of some local religious leaders, teachers, and parents that the law established a religion and violated the freedom of inquiry protected by the First Amendment. Noted scientists from all over the country testified against the law in a ten-day trial that was attended by representatives of over seventy news organizations.

In January of 1982 Judge William Overton issued an opinion declaring the law unconstitutional and making findings of fact and law so strong that proponents of creationism deferred an appeal in favor of pursuing what they hoped would be a more favorable case testing a similar equal-time law in Louisiana. Passing over the plaintiffs' academic freedom claims, the judge ruled that the Arkansas law violated the Establishment Clause of the First Amendment. He took the creationist case apart piece by piece, examined it in light of the nature of science, and reached the conclusion that ". . . 'creation science' as defined in that section [of the act] is simply not science." This would have been enough in itself to bury the claim for equal time, but the court went on to conclude that the purpose and "the *only* real effect of Act

33

590 is the advancement of religion." Not only did the precepts of creation science match the Book of Genesis point for point and lack any educational value as science, "the State failed to produce any evidence which would warrant an inference or conclusion that at any point in the process anyone considered the legitimate educational value of the Act." In sum, Act 590 was "simply and purely an effort to introduce the Biblical version of creation into the public school curriculum."

This finding left two more parts of the creationists' fabric of misunderstanding to be unraveled. The model act, which the creationists are hawking around the country and which Arkansas adopted in 1981, prohibits the teaching of religion, a clause whose purpose, no doubt, is to reinforce the claim that creationism is science. The judge perceived, however, that this requirement set up a situation in which school officials, teachers, and other government officials would constantly have to be evaluating texts, lesson plans, lectures, and library books to determine what was religious and what was scientific. This kind of incessant entanglement of government with religion was found to be clearly prohibited by the separation of church and state provided for in the First Amendment. At the end of his opinion, Judge Overton acknowledged the creationist argument that evolution is a religion no more entitled to be taught in public schools than any other religion: "Assuming for the purposes of argument, however, that evolution is a religion or religious tenet, the remedy is to stop the teaching of evolution; not establish another religion in opposition to it."

In this last aspect of his ruling, the Judge approached, but did not grasp, the underlying argument of the creationists that any basis of knowledge, whether scientific or theistic, is ultimately grounded in belief. In the end, the court ruled that "no group, no matter how large or small, may use the organs of government, of which the public schools are the most conspicuous and influential, to foist its religious beliefs on others." Had the creationists been able to remove the word "religious" from this sentence, they would have given the court a conundrum it plainly does not wish to confront.

The scientific absurdity of the creationist claim makes it too easy to ignore the fact that both the California and the Arkansas cases rest on a struggle between rationality and faith. World views competing for hegemony in American culture are competing in schooling as well. The most significant aspect of the litigation, like the political efforts that are more widespread and more successful, is not the development of legal theory to support or attack the creationist position but the social causes and cultural dislocations that give rise to the contests.

It has been suggested by one study of science textbook controversies that the causes for the renewed attack on evolution by space-age fundamentalists arise primarily from a general social disillusionment with science and an antiauthoritarianism characterized by suspicion toward the arrogance of expertise. Certainly scientists are one class of the priests of explanation whose expertise is increasingly arcane and inaccessible to ordinary people and even to experts in other areas. But there is more to the resurrection of theocracy than an attack on inaccessible expertise.

The scientific creationists, careful to avoid the banner of religion and determined to make use of science itself wherever possible, are nonetheless plainly engaged in an attempt to impose one religious interpretation of the origin of life. Equal-time claims to the contrary notwithstanding, creationists seek to join their belief structure to the power of the state for the purpose of controlling the socialization of children. But the truth of the creationists' claim is that those who adhere to the scientific world view and equate the creationists with the Flat Earth Society are also attempting to control public-school ideology. Each side has tried to avoid appearing to be engaged in a battle for control of public orthodoxy in schools. Both sides have publicly denied that they represent religious or ideological interests and have focused on the "objective truth" of their positions. Each has accused the other of being a value system or a religion while describing itself as value-neutral. No doubt the rational mind will find much more proof for the theory of biological evolution than for a creationist view, which denies the validity of everything from selective breeding to carbon dating. But since the essential conflict is between faith and reason, this proof is quite beside the point.

The claims to objective truth have only driven the controversy deeper into the national psyche; for now the battle seems, in the minds of the antagonists, to be about whether the culture's sources of knowledge (and truth) shall be primarily faith, spirituality, and the revealed word, or rationality, human will, and scientific inquiry. The stakes could hardly be higher than in a contest over the epistemology of a culture; and it is understandable that such a contest would arouse passion, defensiveness, self-righteousness, and fear. Here is a fragment of a speech given by Nell Segraves, one of the plaintiffs in the California creationist litigation:

> One of our main concerns was the way our children were being taught in the schools—they were being taught that they evolved from other creatures rather than created in God's image. It seemed that many of society's problems hinged on this wrong belief. And there were so many problems—I think that is what always scares us, that there are so many problems but seemingly no solutions.

The fear of problems without solutions is really a fear of problems that are not understood and cannot be explained. This lack of acceptable explanations is made vastly more frightening by open conflict over the basis of truth in the culture. In helping to rekindle the contest between science and creationism, Mrs. Segraves has unwittingly pointed to the deeper crisis of collapsed explanations. In a study of "Science Textbook Controversies and the Politics of Equal Time," done by Dorothy Nelkin for the National Science Foundation and the Massachusetts Institute of Technology, the following conclusion was reached:

The recurrence of textbook disputes suggests that the truce between science and religion, based on the assumption that they deal with separate domains, may be a convenient but unrealistic myth. Religion as well as science purports to be a picture of reality, a means through which people render their lives and the world around them intelligible. . . . It is clear that for many people science, often unrelated to their experience, does not serve as a satisfactory explanation of reality on which to base their values. Failing to find a sense of personal integration from scientific beliefs, they seek alternative explanations.

Although the controversy between faith and rationality may not at present involve vast numbers of people in the United States, Nelkin's observation about the personal and cultural depth of this crisis is chilling. Cultural regeneration could be the ultimate result of such a crisis, but the spread of uncertainty about the values that underlie modern culture seems a more likely result. The contest between evolution and creationism centers on which explanation of reality shall be certified by government as valid for the next generation.

5
Casualty List

The search for "alternative explanations" is not restricted to those for whom Darwin is a devil, as the proliferation of other textbook censorship and control issues demonstrates. Given the number of basic issues of personal and cultural consciousness that are being contested in the textbook battles, it is impossible to foresee what ideology or combination of beliefs will win the war over public orthodoxy. Neither the collapse of cultural explanations, which precipitates this war, nor the repression characterized by the attempt to impose explanations politically upon the schools suggests that any resolution is in sight.

Although literature, curriculum, and textbook battles include issues as diverse as the cultural definition of truth, the structure of authority, the significance of gender, racism, religion, and sexuality, indications are that these contests only scratch the surface of school socialization. The public is becoming increasingly aware that schooling is never value-neutral; and, lacking individual alternatives, the public is increasingly interested in controlling the process of value inculcation.

Scholars are becoming increasingly interested in the ways in which this process takes place. Recently, for example, a number of studies of high school history textbooks have demonstrated in considerable detail how the view of American history taught, learned, and evaluated in public schools has reflected some political interests and not others. The most exhaustive study is Frances Fitzgerald's *America Revised*, which documents the changing nature of America's history texts as a function of changes in national politics. Jean Anyon's shorter study, "Ideology and United States History Textbooks," is more pointed in showing that the texts have given a slanted view of labor and economic history, which may have influenced the ability to organize unions among public-school graduates.

Labor unions and other political groups, unlike the right wing and the fundamentalists, have not joined in large scale public battles over the contents of textbooks. But the time cannot be far off when all parts of the political and social spectrum will realize, along with Professor Anyon, that "textbook history illustrates one way of imposing beliefs and constraining choice." Moreover, the parallel collapse of cultural explanations and enhancement of understanding of school socialization will lead the search for alternative explanations to affect not just texts but all aspects of the schools' hidden curriculum that have "contributed to the formation of attitudes that make it easier for powerful groups, those whose knowledge is legitimized by school studies, to manage and control society."

Current cases of textbook censorship and control are already complex. They include opposing parent groups committed to different world views and values and equally determined to have their views prevail in the schools. They also include teachers whose professional identities are called into question by censorship; civil libertarians who struggle to make the First Amendment and the system of freedom of expression apply to compulsory schooling; school boards, which are often caught in a cross fire between groups trying to control or possess them; and children whose curiosity and understanding are often stultified by being made pawns in the ideological wars of adults.

Teachers: The Loss of Morale

The advent of censorship in schools comes at a time when public esteem for teachers is low and their professional self-image is deteriorating. For the nation's teachers, the struggle over public orthodoxy makes a bad situation worse. As the head of one local teachers' association put it after four years of struggling over who would control what went on in the classroom, "Teachers have a tendency to withdraw; they're talkers, not fighters . . . teachers get apathetic, feel rejected . . . their morale is low." The long-term destructive effect of censorship on teachers is observable across the country.

In Levittown, New York, half an hour from Manhattan, one expressive and talented high-school English teacher, recalled his first reactions to the school board's decision that eleven works of fiction by Malamud, Vonnegut, Langston Hughes, Richard Wright, and others would be banned from library and classroom: "One teacher was looking after a class that was not his own when the principal entered the room, walked over to him, and peeling back the left part of his suit jacket to reveal a paperbound copy of Malamud's *The Fixer* under his arm, asked in a hushed, gravelly voice, 'Got any of these?' The teacher assumed that the principal was collecting a set for another English class to use and helped locate three copies around the room. Later we found out the books had been arrested and were being held without bail." According to the English teacher, the episode mirrored others in which books were seized or banned without reason and without any notice, discussion, or due process. It reminded him of Solzhenitsyn's descriptions of the frightening meaninglessness and disorientation that accompanies an arrest by secret police.

In the years since these book arrests, the English teacher has been unable to figure out why the censorship occurred and whether it might not occur again without warning. For a

40

year afterward, the English department was unable to decide on replacement books for fear of violating some unknowable boundary of propriety. "It got so we were saying 'we can't have a book with a Jew in it. . . .' We thought of using *Barabbas,* but that was too Christian. . . ." The trauma of censorship was never far from this teacher's mind in spite of his continued good humor: "If we do this, will we get stomped on?"

In Warsaw, Indiana, a less seasoned, but equally talented and committed high-school teacher, Teresa Burnau, understood clearly the struggle in which she and her professional judgment became the lightning rod for antifeminist, fundamentalist discontent and secular power seeking. She never came to terms with the fact that the academic freedom and openness of inquiry she had been taught to believe in and practice could be made a public offense by the democratic process. She could not lose the feeling of being the unexpected and irrationally chosen victim: "You see, when I am forced to deal with the situation as it continues, even thinking about it, I become horribly afraid. The fear controls me. I don't want to talk to strangers. I can't even go into stores I've never been in. I perceive anything unfamiliar as a threat." The antifeminist censors in Warsaw, Indiana, also perceived anything unfamiliar as a threat; and they have temporarily succeeded in transmitting this part of their world view to the teachers over whose shoulders they are looking.

In the California town of Anderson, a few hours north of the laid-back cosmopolitanism of San Francisco, V. I. Wexner left his high-school teaching job for writing and farming. He had been hassled out of a generally successful role as the teacher who got high-school students interested in reading literature. His classroom was a library of all kinds of books which had proved their ability to attract readers from among those who never cared much for reading. Wexner was turning television watchers into book readers. His mistake was to order books by Richard Brautigan. Titles such as *The Pill versus the Springhill Mine Disaster* and *The Abortion: An Historical Romance* caught the eye of a principal concerned with local opposition to family planning or sex education. The books were initially judged by their covers, but pretty soon all of the Brautigan books in Wexner's reading room save two were on the way out as smut. It was a full decade since the board had banned Salinger's *Catcher in the Rye*.

Wexner's practice had always been to instruct students not to continue reading anything they found offensive and to consult with their parents about any questionable books. But parental control over their own children's reading was not enough to satisfy the righteous of Anderson, one of whom wrote in a local letter to the editor: "The only education they [banned books] would be 'sound' for is if we are planning to turn out a generation of prostitutes and sex deviates." Wexner was as much the victim of his fellow teachers as of local book vigilantes. He had espoused and practiced a philosophy of teaching that other teachers could not afford to accept.

One teacher attacked Wexner publicly for being "antiauthority" and running a class without anyone else telling him what to do. In spite of a clear willingness to let parents make reading decisions for their children, parents accused Wexner of "trying desperately to make it so that there is no authority governing anything in his classroom. If he wins this case he will have really put himself in a position where nobody could touch him."

Wexner saw the issue not as one of alleged pornography but as one of competing images of what it meant to be a teacher in a public school. The irony of being attacked by colleagues was not lost on him: "Most of the attacks on me came from the faculty. . . . I'd just written a lot of these people off as square or out-of-it; but then it began to dawn on me that from their point of view they were in a holy war, and I was an enemy of the state."

The state's view of teaching was held not just by the teachers it tolerated but by the administration of the school. Wexner wrote, "I knew the principal had a fetish about the chain of command, but I thought that was because he was a bully. I didn't see it then as part of a nationwide pattern. It's frightening. I obviously picked a bad time to be defending freedom of choice and the rights of those low down in the hierarchy."

Teachers like Wexner and Burnau must continually make complex judgments, balancing their academic concerns with the interests and needs of their pupils, the parents, the school administration, and the majority of citizens in the district. This process ceases to be individual and professional and becomes politicized by censorship conflicts that reflect the broad cultural concerns and narrow power interests of the community. A national survey of 2,000 teachers by the National Council of Teachers of English shows that over 30 percent have had experiences with censorship. The result of these experiences from the point of view of the teachers is de-professionalizing and demoralizing.

The most palpable atmosphere created by censorship is a climate of fear. Students have observed that "it's too bad they [teachers] are so scared they can't let their talents out." Elsewhere an ex-New York cop who was narrowly defeated in an attempt to unseat a procensorship school-board member on Long Island knew why "not one single English teacher would step forward" as plaintiff in a free-speech suit. "People's jobs are on the line; and teachers are a dime a dozen," he said.

Teachers are not simply afraid of the consequences of resisting censorship; they are censoring themselves, growing less confident about their own professional judgment, and becoming so insecure that they have trouble talking to each other about their reactions to censorship. Isolation and even the hostility of colleagues are fear's companions. State and national teachers' unions have been reluctant to support those fighting censorship, apparently aware of how easily bargaining agents and whole professions can become the objects of witch hunting.

The suddenly shifting standards of teaching, which are the result of repeated battles for control of books and curriculum, focus teachers away from their students and even their students' families toward powerful but unpredictable political forces. Teachers who are predisposed to consult with families about class plans find the relationships polarized. Both sides become defensive. Compromises in which teachers seek parental approval for reading materials are often blocked. As a result, teachers may look increasingly up the bureaucratic chain of command for administrative controls. Here they often find, as they did in Warsaw Indiana, that they have no meaningful forum for their professional input about book selection because all semblance of consultation and due process has been swept away by public hysteria over unpopular values.

If the fear, uncertainty, and kaleidoscopic demands bred by censorship isolate teachers from their students' families, from their own professional standards and organizations, and from the school hierarchy, they have cast a pall over the teacher-student relationship.

One East Coast teacher knows from personal experience that *Go Ask Alice,* the depressing autobiography of a teenage girl whose involvement with drugs leads to her death, has turned some kids off drugs; yet the parents want the book banned because they fear it will corrupt children. Communication on this subject between teacher and student is disrupted by parental literal-mindedness.

In the Midwest, a tenured English teacher refused to respond to a student's question because she "might get fired" if she did. Within two hours the superintendent of schools knew about the remark and had the teacher directed not to discuss such things with her students.

Teachers begin to fear that some students will report a minor incident out of context to a parent who will then precipitate a political disruption of the classroom. In Levittown, New York, a single half-frame picture of an intrauterine device on a film strip followed this route to a requirement that every audio-visual aid in the school system be catalogued and that none be used unless it appeared in the catalogue. Students see the self-protective isolationism of fearful teachers as apathy and wonder why the teachers are not more interested in students. Are the teachers there just to make a buck and go home? they ask.

The teacher/student relationship, like the relationships between doctor and patient and priest and penitent, is a delicate one; and like these relationships, important to the society as well as the individual participants. The learning connection, especially when the students are young, is easily rigidified and snapped. This relationship needs the same protection society offers to other "privileged" relationships if any semblance of trust and subtlety is to be preserved and if schooling is to be anything more than a "twelve-year sentence."

When teachers and students feel they can no longer be interested in one another or fear expressing themselves or think they must examine every question and answer for signs that curiosity may trespass orthodoxy, teaching and learning lose their connection. Under such circumstances teaching becomes bureaucratized, learning is distorted by coercion, and schools become nothing more than political battlegrounds and institutions for the inefficient management of children's time. The struggles over textbooks and curriculum taking place around the country expose teachers and students to tensions, fears, and manipulation, which can only worsen the already bleak prospects for useful education in public schools. It is ironic that such nihilistic consequences should flow from the actions of parents who believe that the schools do not develop the values the parents respect.

At the base of the dilemma that censorship creates for teachers is a conflict between two images of the teacher's role in public schooling as it is presently structured. One image, drawn from the days of tutorial education and from traditional concepts of higher education, is that teachers exercise independent professional judgment about intellectual, pedagogical, and value matters in the classroom. Because the students are underage, the exercise of this professional judgment requires taking into account the values and cultural assumptions of the children's families. As children approach high school, this image of the teacher's role is perceived to mean that students should be exposed to a variety of ideas and values and that wherever possible the classroom should be a marketplace of ideas.

The second, competing, image of the teacher in public school is a product of the general institutionalization of life. The teacher becomes the agent of the administrative hierarchy, which in turn owes its allegiance to whatever passes for the local political majority. The school is in *loco parentis* for the local community's composite parent. The values that inform the hiring, direction, and firing of teachers as well as the selection texts and programs are the values that the majority of the community is comfortable with. The reality of socialization as part of schooling from kindergarten through twelfth grade is recognized by making the definition of that socialization—of the transmission of culture—depend upon the political control of the school system. The teacher as independent professional becomes the teacher as bureaucratic agent.

There is substantial confusion, uncertainty, and disagreement about which of these two images should operate in the public schools. The teachers themselves do not agree; and the censorship struggles have created a situation in which the law is being asked to establish one or the other image as official, enforceable reality. As contests of power directed at the establishment of orthodoxy in the schools, struggles over censorship assume the agent/bureaucrat model of teaching.

In the cases currently before the federal courts, school boards that have been attacked for stifling free expression defend themselves by insisting that they have the legitimate power to socialize children according to community standards. In *Pico* v. *Board of Education,* the Levittown, New York, case involving Malamud, Vonnegut, and other novelists, the Board of Education argued that "a principal function of all elementary and secondary education is indoctrination . . . to transmit the basic values of the community

. . . in secondary school a prescriptive, inculcative or indoc-trinative process applies."

The board was able to quote various legal scholars who take a similarly jaundiced view of the role of teachers and the structure of schooling:

> [Teacher control of curriculum] is at clear variance with the historically accepted societal view that the deliberate in-culcation of the right societal values is a major function of American public education.
>
> —(Goldstein)

> The secondary school . . . acts in loco parentis . . . It is closely governed by a local community. The faculty does not have independent traditions, the broad discretion as to teaching methods, nor usually the intellectual qualifica-tions, of university professors. Among secondary school teachers there are often many persons with little experi-ence. Some teachers and most students have limited intel-lectual and emotional maturity.
>
> —*Mailloux* v. *Kiley* 323 F.Supp. 1392

The teachers know well enough what majority control of schooling decisions means though they are unaccustomed to hearing insults used to justify this arrangement. Shown the board's brief in *Pico,* one local teacher simply exclaimed, "I am not a teaching machine." Some of the parents in the same town recognize that as distasteful as it may be to teachers to be forced to adopt such an agent/bureaucrat image of their work, it is the way schools run. In the words of one woman, "The prevailing view of the teacher's role is as an agent of a school board running schools like hotels."

Many teachers, like those of Anderson, California, seem to have already internalized this role and to be willing to attack any of their colleagues, such as V. I. Wexner, who as-sert the contrary. Still other teachers seem not to know what to think of their role. They are caught between a desire for professional independence and respect and the fear of losing their jobs if they actually act as professionals. In Teresa Burnau's case an early discussion with the attorney for the state teachers' association led her to indicate that she would take a reduced monetary settlement if the school board would insert an academic freedom clause in the next teachers' contract. The attorney's response was, "What's an academic freedom clause?" Clearly the professional image of public-school teachers does not have the same currency as the agency image.

Some organizations, such as the NCTE and the American Civil Liberties Union, have argued that academic freedom is inherent in public-school teaching. They assert the professional role of teachers, confident that teachers can deal individually with parents about values if they can avoid dealing collectively with the political majority. But the reality of the teachers' position in an era of declining enrollments and the perpetual battles over value orthodoxy in schools make this an unlikely development. They are simply too vulnerable to be able to do much creative and forceful thinking about what their role should be. And virtually none of them have been able to take account of the inevitability of socialization in schools in formulating a clear definition of the professional teacher's relationship to individual families and community majorities.

The head of the teachers' association in the district involved in the *Pico* case claims that "a teacher's class is his or her own domain." He thinks that the students and the books will survive the censorship struggles but that the teachers will be the real losers because of "the danger that the agent/bureaucrat role will take hold" as a result of censorship. Some legal scholars have seen an emphasis on the teacher's right to determine what to teach as a substantial countervailing weight to censorship. But none of these scholars, teachers, or parents have figured out how to make an individual liberty such as academic freedom meaningful when families are virtually compelled to send their children to schools controlled by political majorities. In order to take account of school socialization, the rights of parents to influence the values children are taught, and the professional image of a teacher's role, majority control of schooling will have to be reexamined. No one, least of all beleaguered teachers dependent on the current configuration of this $100 billion-a-year industry, is ready for that. Meanwhile, the image of teacher as tool of the political majority looms larger and larger over the public schools.

The School Board: A Double Bind for the Willing Servant

Censorship battles polarize school districts, creating the illusion of certainty among people struggling with confusion and alienation, sharpening apparent value differences, and bringing a climate of fear and recrimination into classroom and community. The school board is expected to defuse this tension and to create cohesion out of conflict. It is a job as futile as reconciling competing theologies. When Ivan Illich pointed out that "the school is becoming the established church of secular times" he might have been read by school-board members in the United States as issuing a warning that it would be next to impossible for the school-board member to avoid becoming a grand inquisitor.

How should a school board deal with censorship, the selection of teaching materials, and the control of curriculum? The board owes its allegiance, by appointment or election, to the majority. It is faced with the political expression of competing values, which are at once deeply personal and broadly cultural in nature. Pulled and tugged by the agents of public orthodoxy to take a partisan stand but prohibited by the structure of compulsory schooling from creating a system of voluntary family choice of alternative schools, the board is expected to choose victors *and* to mediate among the contenders. Neither position is workable. The board cannot end the conflict disrupting the schools except by going out of business; the board's existence as the expression of majority control is required if the battle over public orthodoxy is to proceed.

49

Though the board may perceive itself as being caught unarmed in the middle of a political cross fire, there is more to it. Ideology, like power, abhors a vacuum. If the culture's explanations have collapsed, causing doubt about what children will grow up to believe about the world and how they will behave, then the board is expected to fashion a new community cohesion. It becomes the school board's job to save the children from the alienation and anxiety of their elders. Without even adequate political tools, the school board is being asked to solve cultural problems.

Of course, the nation has its share of school boards that are not only unconcerned with the dangers of politically imposed orthodoxy but are the energetic allies or even initiators of censorship. Sometimes school-board members attend state or local conferences where hit lists of objectionable books are distributed along with page and paragraph references that enable them to know just what is wrong with a book without having to bother reading it. Parents who receive mailings from any of the scores of state and national groups whose aim is to sanitize library and curriculum often find a school-board member who will join forces with them. Detailed examinations of the politics of censorship have shown that there are significant, if temporary, political gains to be made by school-board members willing to express the anger of citizens frustrated by an illegible culture and an insensitive school system.

School boards that are not collusively involved in censorship efforts are typically unprepared to deal with them. There are four responses available to the board looking for a way to defuse apparently irreconcilable conflict over text or curriculum: compromise, judgment based upon educational criteria that are neutral as to content, due process in the handling of competing claims, and the idea of the classroom as a marketplace of ideas. For various reasons, none of these responses is satisfactory.

Compromise is often contrary to the interests of the parties to the conflict. To begin with, many people who seek the elimination or inclusion of books or curriculum want to use the schools to impose their values upon the entire population. They may wish to remove what they label pornography or want to excise sexual or racial stereotypes; they may want to exorcise a devil, or they may be agents of absolute morality. At bottom, though, they wish to protect their own children, and winning these ends is not enough to contain their anxiety. They wish to save the whole new generation. They do not like their children being taught anyone else's ideology with tax money, and eventually they become so righteous they see no reason why the public should resist paying for *their* ideology.

The attempts of teachers to resolve conflicts over books before they reach the banning stage provides further evidence that compromise does not accomplish the goals the combatants have in mind. In a number of situations teachers have proposed that only those children whose parents consent should read and study a book that has become controversial. School librarians, who are often the focus of censorship, have proposed that controversial literature be placed on special shelves where only family consent will provide student access. These suggestions have been turned aside not only by parents who seek orthodoxy before self-protection but by school principals and superintendents who realize that a witch hunt is not a witch hunt unless the witches are publicly attacked and excluded from the community.

In many instances compromise is structurally impossible. If the board is choosing one reading textbook for grade two, that book shows girls and women either in domestic roles only or in all work roles. Two sets of books cannot be purchased, and the composite image of gender won't be acceptable to at least one side of the controversy. The creation of state-wide criteria for textbooks—such as those of California, which is 10 percent of the national school textbook market—often becomes extraordinarily detailed in its prescription of approved content. The compromises reached at this level are often totally artificial and satisfy no one, thus continuing the conflict. California's decade-long struggle

51

over creationism and evolution in approved social science and biology texts is an example.

Judgment of text and curriculum based solely upon "educational criteria" that do not deal with ideological content is often proposed but has yet to take on any reality. Because so many of the censorship controversies seem to be based upon the arbitrary preferences of one group or another, "educational criteria" are seen as a way of neutralizing the censors. These criteria resurrect the expertise of school officials and seem to insulate them from parents who cannot compete on a professional level.

Teachers who describe their methods of choosing books lend credence to the educational criteria approach by pointing out that they choose books on the basis of whether they are teachable, interesting to students, appropriate to their age and intellectual maturity. One legal brief written on behalf of parents resisting the removal of books claims that school boards should bear the burden of presenting an educationally justifiable reason for removing a book, or else the court should rule that "instead of serving an educational purpose . . . the school board's action related solely to the social and political tastes of school board members."

Aside from the fact that none of the purportedly neutral educational criteria have really been articulated, the problem with this response to censorship is that it ignores the legitimate interests of the conflicting parties. However polarizing the tactics or effects of censorship may be, there is a level on which the complaining parents are in fact trying to arrange a sound education for their children. The values of these parents are violated by what they perceive to be going on in school, and they are entitled both to hold those values and to seek their extension to their children. The right of parents to influence the upbringing and education of their children cannot be successfully shunted aside with arcane discussions of pedagogy and child development.

If there are in the school "educational criteria" that do not deal with these parents' values, the parents are not concerned with them. Just at the point at which there ought to be a strengthening of the relationship between family and teacher, trying to professionalize issues would only add to the destructive isolation of parents from their concerns. The spread of censorship as a form of parental demand for influence over the schools indicates that parents are becoming too sophisticated and too energized to be shunted aside by an extra dose of professionalism.

Due process would appear to be the most promising way to transform book-banning binges into sane discussions of educational policy. The trouble with due-process response to censorship, even if it were implemented, is that while it may cool some tempers and quiet some false indignation, it provides no guidance about how to reconcile the conflicting value positions of people who want the schools to move in very different directions. Censorship remains a conflict of belief and world view, which at times can be so deep that it defies reconciliation. As with religious beliefs, perhaps such differences of values are an inappropriate subject for reconciliation by public political processes. This is not an argument against due process. In areas from television regulation to criminal trials, due process has proved to be essential to fair decision making, even though it does not provide substantive guidelines. But due-process assurances of fairness, no matter how sensitive, do not remove the school board from its dilemma, as may be seen from imagining the effect of due process on a censorship controversy.

Suppose that a group of parents approaches a school board with the demand that a number of books be eliminated from the curriculum and the library because they expose children to values unacceptable to the community. After making all manner of accusations about invasions of family privacy, encouragment of drug use and promiscuity, filth, smut and violation of religious scruples, the parents succeed in having the board ban the books, effective immediately. No parents with opposing views are heard, and no teacher is asked to explain how the books are used or to evaluate the educational value of the books. None of the school-board members have read the books. A small group of parents who are offended both by the tactics of the censors and by the results they achieve brings suit, claiming, among other things, that minority viewpoint parents were deprived of due process, and therefore the board could not have made a reasonable decision. The court agrees and tells the board that it must reconsider the issue on the basis of its previously adopted policy of hearings, evidence, argument, and professional advice. What is the result?

Assume that the board complies with the judge's order, and a reasonable discussion takes place. In the more careful atmosphere the parent majority becomes more ideologically articulate, detailing how the challenged books create a pattern of beliefs that sanction antiauthoritarianism, denigrate girls who aspire to be housewives and mothers, and promote pacifism, collectivism, and antitheism. The books and their use in the curriculum are alleged to represent official support of moral relativism.

Opposing parents are equally articulate in their claim that these values are valid and useful in modern society; that the contents of books do not determine the beliefs and behavior of children; that majority parents seek to impose an orthodoxy upon public schools by banning dissenting views from the socialization process; and that the books are reputable texts and literature of proven educational value. If the board then decides that the books are not appropriate and should be eliminated from the curriculum and library because they trespass the values of a majority of the families in the community, has the conflict been resolved?

The offensive tone of the controversy has been eliminated, but the result is still the banning of books and the stigmatizing of beliefs some parents hold sincerely and want communicated to their children. Whether the board's second decision is called "textbook selection" or "censorship," it chooses some values over others and takes a step in making the school socialization process the transmitter of some world views and the stigmatizer of others. The victory of the apparent majority is not likely to be tolerated for long by those who feel their children's consciousness is now being manipulated in a negative direction.

The fourth response available to school-board members faced with the onset of the censorship plague is to attempt to include all value positions advocated by any parents, making the school system a "marketplace of ideas." The phrase is borrowed from a concept of freedom of expression by which every adult is assured the right to express opinions, hear them from others, and participate in the unfettered formulation of everything from public policy to personal consciousness. But the idea that public schools, like the society at large, should be a place for open and noncoercive exchanges of views is more honorable than it is realistic. It appears from the examination of dozens of school censorship cases that virtually no school-board members hold this concept of schooling or argue for its adoption. Its only remote referent is in the numbing and watered-down curriculum called "least common denominator." It is usually left to the attorneys for dissenting parents to make the claim for open and vigorous inquiry in public schools. Most school-board members cannot contradict the argument of parents or of the history of schooling, both of which recognize public schools as a thirty hours per week substitute for the child-rearing function of families.

The marketplace of ideas concept is considerably more practical at the high school than the elementary school level. As children approach the more complete development of their intellectual faculties and emotional security, it makes more sense to believe that they should be exposed to new ideas and values and learn to know themselves and the world through a process of evaluating conflicting views of reality. The same could hardly be said for the second grader. A conflict model of child rearing for every age level rings with misunderstanding of children and parents. This makes schools operating from such a model unsatisfactory childcare institutions.

The marketplace concept also ignores the reality of

schooling as an institution. Institutions, even ones that are not total institutions, have a structure, rules, role models, and, in the case of schools, books and teaching materials, which affect both the behavior and beliefs of people in those institutions. Providing equal time for contrasting viewpoints or ideas touches only the surface of the social milieu. The "hidden curriculum" has come to be recognized by education researchers as well as parents as a major source of socialization of children. The clear merit of avoiding overt, direct manipulations of consciousness does not substantially reduce the degree to which schools socialize children.

The marketplace concept is at best a partial response applicable to high-school students who can, and often do, assert their rights not to be pawns in any group's well-intentioned effort to "save" them. But this response can also be the tool of groups wishing to maintain power over school socialization at all levels. The ringing call for freedom to teach and learn is often sounded by education professionals as a counterbalance to the right wing.

The argument that many censors were part of an interlocking right-wing directorate whose political goals extended far beyond control of curriculum was advanced with considerable evidence in a review of school censorship from World War II through the late fifties. The same argument, with fresh evidence, is now being made about the current proliferation of censorship. In an article appearing in the *Phi Delta Kappan* and reprinted in a book entitled *Dealing with Censorship*, Charles Park presents the evidence for believing that a significant part of the current censorship is a manifestation of an organized "new right." He concludes that "the evidence reflects with startling clarity that right-wing interests have found the public schools a convenient target for unifying ultra-conservative ideology and traditional morality for political gain." Certainly the values of many parents support the idea that the right provides a lightning rod for public discontent and confusion. As Park points out, "The argument is advanced that when education is presented without reference to the truth as given by God, the schools in effect teach students to become atheists . . . The themes are illustrative of a values conflict in which the New Right asserts that truth is revealed and that education must not be a vehicle for allowing an individual to explore ideas independently, but rather to accept without question established truths by selected authorities. The dimensions of this conflict suggest the need for renewed educational concern about academic freedom."

With arguments like these and even more urgent claims that any attack on the policies of public schools is the product of an organized right-wing effort, the stage is set for the marketplace of ideas to become the rallying point of all freedom lovers. The problem with this approach is not simply that it oversimplifies the complex and diverse sources of censorship—left and right, black and white, establishment and counterculture; it demeans parents whose concern for their own values and their children's extends to public-school policy. In this context the marketplace position becomes a robe of secular sanctity under which school officials can hide. The marketplace concept can be used to deny the inevitable socialization function of schools and to disclaim the plain fact that school boards and professional educators already prescribe that children shall "accept without question established truths by selected authorities."

The difference between the censors and those who cry "marketplace" is often simply one of ideology, however sincere and honorable the advocates of diversity in public schools may be. Jonathan Kozol's study of how the children of the well-to-do are educated in public schools reveals some of the ideology and socialization that the marketplace concept obscures or makes undiscussable. Kozol finds that "the containment of youth, which lies at the heart of school indoctrination, depends upon the demolition of a child's ideological and ethical perceptions . . ." Some of the parts of the established ideology of public schools, which Kozol uncovers with pained eloquence, include the inoculation of the young "against vigorous response" to the exploitation that is the common lot of most of the world; "ethical numbness"; "the myth of progress"; the "inability to say no"; the belief that no one bears responsibility for suffering and that "there are no victims" in the world and therefore no victimizers. As Kozol has seen it, it is not the right wing or the Christian fundamentalists who aim to "kill off the conscience of the rich," but those who hold the reigns of power now.

> Most of all we might grow up without the shell, the casement . . . that protects us from . . . visible action on those evils we perceive. We might grow up to be brave and subversive human beings. It is against this ever-present danger that twelve years in public school protect us.

Arguments that schools should be a "marketplace of ideas" are not particularly useful in ending pitched conflict over censorship. These arguments create the illusion that schooling can be value neutral and obscure the values that are already the subject of the institutionalized indoctrination of children. As a result of the lack of utility of this and other responses a school board might make to censorship, the most sincere, sensitive, and honorable persons in charge of public schooling have the unenviable and impossible task of dealing with value conflicts in which emotion is high and personal and cultural stakes are increasing. The responses they have available to them are meagre at best. Worst of all is the dimly perceived possibility that no public servant, however willing, ought to be called upon to fashion cohesive community values where they plainly do not exist and where the attempt to do so is itself a major source of conflict.

Children: Growing Up with Censorship

Censorship can be viewed not only as an attempt by adults to inject meaning into a fragmented culture but as an attempt to save the children from whatever the adults fear. By the time these children are old enough to have reasonably independent intellects, one wants to know whether they distinguish what is being done *for* them from what is being done *to* them.

When the Amish community of Wisconsin successfully convinced the Supreme Court that compulsory high-school attendance was an unconstitutional infringement on the community's religious values and practices, Justice William O. Douglas wondered, "If the parents . . . are allowed a religious exemption, the inevitable effect is to impose the parents' notions of religious duty upon their children. Where the child is mature enough to express potentially conflicting desires, it would be an invasion of the child's rights to permit such an imposition without canvassing his views . . . the child has no other effective forum . . ."

At some point children cease being members of a family unit, which has the recognized role of maintaining and transmitting values, and become individuals capable of perceiving whether they are the pawns of a politicized struggle over culture. At this point a new element may be added to the censorship conflict: the students' desire to influence their own education. Sorting out the rights of parents and children will be complex but will not be seriously addressed until the rights of parents and the political majority are adjusted.

In districts engaged in long-term struggles over book and curriculum control, the perceptions of high-school students suggest the outlines of the effect of growing up with censorship. A self-protective apathy—the "shell" that Kozol perceives as insulating the young from their own reaction to reality—is the prevailing, though by no means exclusive, reaction of high-school students to censorship.

One California teacher in the thick of a censorship battle observed that "the people who fight are in their forties and fifties. The kids are indifferent and don't see it as a public issue—they see it as bad but do nothing—other teachers froth up their students [to support censorship]." Halfway across the country a group of twelve sixteen- and seventeen-year-olds was able to gather only 200 signatures on a petition opposing censorship and book burning in a high school with over 1,200 students. None of the students had ever read about or had discussed in class either the function of civil liberty in America or the historical threats to liberty such as the Red Scare of the Twenties or McCarthyism.

There is a practical justification for the outward show of apathy. "My parents," said one seventeen-year-old girl, "tell me not to get involved. They say, 'We have to live in this community!'" On Long Island five high-school students carried the burden of asserting the students' right to read. One observed that "most of the kids don't care one way or the other."

The passivity, myopia, and fear-induced apathy of most students cannot be attributed solely to the battles over orthodoxy taking place around them. These reactions are related to the mass-production model of learning that pervades the entire school experience. Students are not supposed to react critically to what the authorities teach them. Those who understand the closely controlled system of rewards and punishments that is public school know that the survivors—those who graduate as good students—are generally the ones who keep their heads down, follow directions, and profess to believe what they are told to believe. But censorship is seen by these outwardly apathetic students as a part of school that is consistent with the machine-made message of passivity they confront daily. They see themselves as marking time while adults fight over power and fiddle with the schools. They know a battle is being fought over schools in which children have no role except as the passive recipients of the spoils.

The student apathy that meets censorship in schools seems to contain an anger, a fear, and an insecurity about the future. It takes a strong dose of external "order" and a heavy layer of internal apathy to contain these emotions; and it is hard to come away from a discussion with these students without feeling that they could explode in any direction if the conditions changed. In the battle over censorship, it is even possible to imagine that angry, fearful, and confused parents recreate themselves in these children and set the stage for another generation's struggle over orthodoxy in schools. Parental ambiguity about personal power and social order is reflected in the work of professional censors who advise, provoke, and take political power from local parent groups. In one mimeographed review distributed by Education Analysis of Longview, Texas, the following criticism of a teaching manual appears:

> Punk Takes a Stand. Using Creative Dramatics . . . Punk's problem should remind pupils of similar experiences when they had to 'take a stand.' Encourage the pupils to interpret these experiences through creative dramatics. OB-JECTION: No wonder students are 'taking a stand' today! They're being encouraged to in their textbooks!

This is the same group that is pleased at its national success in getting parents to begin caring about how their children are educated and taking a stand for moral values in schooling.

A spirited minority of high-school students do take a stand against the politicized attempts to manipulate their consciousness, claiming a right to direct their own reading and learning; supporting teachers who become the arbitrary victims of censorship campaigns; running the substantial personal risk of having their student newspapers banned; being hassled in school, ostracized in the community, or sentenced to academic capital punishment—expulsion. They do not want to conceive of themselves as the product of any socialization process or as the pawns of any power struggle; and they are willing to fight about it.

In Anderson, California, where a teacher and a publisher fought the banning of five of Richard Brautigan's novels from a classroom library, Ray Thomas, sixteen, spoke out against his history teacher. Thomas took a class examination in February 1980 along with the other students in his class. Thomas was marked wrong on three true-false questions: (1) The Russians believe they can defeat the U.S. in a nuclear war; (2) A coalition government means surrender to the totalitarian government; and (3) Social Security is a giant rip-off.

Thomas wasn't pleased to be penalized for believing that Social Security is not a rip-off. Neither did he like the teacher's comment that President Carter is a "semiretarded peanut farmer," nor his presentation as fact of such ideas as "The UN openly proclaims its chief objective is to bring about a one-world government where Christianity would be prohibited." According to Thomas he is "just exercising my rights" and has "no idea what he may give his biased opinions on." And he never knew precisely which opinions of the teacher might lead him to mark students down for disagreeing with him.

Ray Thomas was fighting a form of censorship more subtle than book banning. He was fighting the use of grades, examinations, and the power of teaching to force students to confess belief in views they do not share. Ray Thomas's parents backed him, but they have been much less successful than the parents who want Brautigan's "filthy" literature removed from the reading shelf.

Brooke Zykan was a student at Warsaw High School in north central Indiana when the school board, under parental pressure, decided to ban five books, fire three teachers, terminate the student newspaper, and eliminate nine elective literature courses from the curriculum. Like some of her friends and classmates, Zykan felt "intellectually dragged down" by the stifling effect the censorship had on her teachers. In a statement made to the Warsaw school board, Zykan spoke for 200 students who "have the feeling we're being suppressed" and who demanded that the board "give us back our academic and intellectual freedom of choice." She shared Studs Terkel's perception of the effect of censorship on children as "a new kind of child abuse perpetrated by persons who are terrified with life and literature and want to pass the fear on to their children."

Unable to move a school board locked into the politics of local power and fundamentalist theology, Brooke Zykan became a plaintiff in a federal suit seeking to restore the banned books, courses, and teachers. Although she had been able to generate signatures on her petition, she was the only student who had the personal courage and family support to become a plaintiff. In her statement before the federal district court, Zykan spoke from personal experience about "the climate of fear and intimidation at Warsaw High School," telling the court that "students must attend class in an environment of administrative surveillance." She described the deteriorating relationship between students and teachers and claimed that censorship had caused her "ability to learn, openly to express opinions, and to reflect creatively on material presented in class" all to suffer.

Steve Pico is another of the growing number of students who, with the help of civil liberties lawyers or student rights organizations, is willing to resist censorship. For Pico the battle to defend the right to read authors like Malamud, Eldridge Cleaver, Hughes, and Vonnegut has become a preoccupation. He has graduated from college and has yet to see the end of the case in which he is a plaintiff and which has enveloped and polarized his hometown of 60,000 in Island Trees, New York.

Pico has worked on the case consistently for four years. He takes his interpretation of censorship from a line in *The Fixer,* one of the banned books: "There are no wrong books . . . ; what's wrong is the fear of them." It is the fear of ideas that Pico sees gripping the predominantly white, Catholic, middle-class suburb of New York City. Pico cannot square this fear with his own attitude that books and ideas "allow people to play out their fantasies" and to become more secure in their values "by comparing them to others." Pico is typical of those students who appear to be much less confused about values and culture than those adults whose certitude takes the form of demands for censorship. For him, the high school is constitutionally compelled to be run as a marketplace of ideas; a formulation he has no doubt is consistent with the power of school boards to socialize children so long as they do not do so by the complete exclusion of any idea.

Unlike the censors, who he feels "act in an attempt to capture what is lost," Pico is too turned on to what is yet to be found to worry about the anxieties of alienated adults. His enormous energy for a prolonged battle seems to depend on his belief that there are no irreconcilable value differences in modern American culture and that majority controlled school boards can be legitimate architects of community cohesion if only they will remain calm.

High-school students in districts plagued by censorship are a good deal more insightful and intelligent than they are given credit for by the censors. Even those who have adopted the protective coloration of apathy see the fear and anxiety of adults. But the most active students are as centered on their own values as the censors are on theirs. Each is unable to transcend his or her own position for long enough to consider what might happen if school socialization were the province of family or individual consent rather than political coercion. Perhaps if the war over public-school orthodoxy subsided and each side could lay aside the need to fight the other, the energy of the conflict and the identity it provides would be lost.

6

One-Eyed Man in the Land of the Blind

With parents, political groups, and censors of all imaginable persuasions and beliefs trying to gain control of public schools on behalf of their own conceptions of truth and right living, it is hardly surprising that civil libertarians have entered the fray. Dissent is under attack; and the traditional watchdogs of individual liberty have found themselves in scores of state and federal courts in an attempt to make the First Amendment relevant to the nation's public schools. In these legal battles, civil libertarians, unlike the censors themselves, see that censorship threatens the system of freedom of expression upon which democracy depends. What they cannot, or will not, see is that schooling without individual family choice must always violate these same civil liberties. Civil libertarians see with one eye while others are blind.

The First Amendment's string of seemingly separate civil liberties—the right of free speech, press, assembly, and religion—protects adults against the imposition of opinion in any form by the government. Were it otherwise, the "just consent of the governed" would be a meaningless concept. The importance of this system of freedom of expression to

American character and politics was underscored by the Supreme Court in the flag salute case decided while Hitler and Mussolini were gobbling up half the world in the name of facism:

> If there is any fixed star in our constitutional constellation, it is that no official, high or petty, can prescribe what shall be orthodox in politics, nationalism, religion, or other matters of opinion or force citizens to confess by word or act their faith therein.
>
> —*Barnette* vs. *West Va.* (1943)

The problem for civil libertarians has been to apply this concept of freedom to the public schools—institutions in which attendance in compulsory, curriculum is controlled, and children rather than adults make up the audience. The task of defending the right to dissent in an institution committed to the expression and transmission of community cohesion is formidable.

Some defenders of public schools believe that the First Amendment can provide little help in dealing with censorship. David Seeley, president of the Public Education Association, has written, "Where in the equation of 'free speech in the schools' do we put . . . parents' fundamental right to raise and educate their children according to their own values? . . . Waving the flag of free speech and the First Amendment and shouting 'censorship' doesn't answer it."

The courts, on the other hand, have made it clear that the First Amendment does apply within the public schools, though with what effect is unclear. In 1969 the Supreme Court ruled that high-school students had the right to peaceful expression of unpopular opinion by wearing black armbands to school to protest the war in Vietnam: "In our system, state operated schools may not be enclaves of totalitarianism . . . [students] may not be regarded as closed-circuit recipients of only that which the state chooses to communicate. They may not be confined to the expression of those sentiments that are officially approved." The case had affirmed the rights of the students only insofar as they did not cause a disruption of order within the school. Since the school authorities remained in control of the closeness with which such order is defined, the Court in fact granted as much to the school board's power to control expression as to the students' right of dissent.

The same dilemma of balancing the power to socialize against the freedom of personal consciousness arises in censorship cases. As Lawrence Tribe, one of the nation's leading constitutional scholars, observed in connection with the armband case: "Since schools are expressly permitted, indeed even created, to promote the very same lessons in the classroom which they are prohibited from dispensing by shibboleth and coerced ceremony, the allocation of power and control in the educational system has been the object of frequent struggles among groups and individuals within the community, each advancing its own meaning of 'liberty' adequate to sustain its own authority and generally conflicting with that of others."

It is not easy to make liberty and compulsory education consistent with one another. School boards and administrators in the dozens of censorship cases now in the courts have claimed an absolute and limitless discretion to control schools and "transmit community values." Unfortunately, in an attempt to find some reasonable limitations on this power, civil libertarians have found themselves creating and relying on concepts that do everything but address the central contradiction between the structure of schooling and the meaning of individual liberty.

The advocates of freedom of expression have found it impossible to ignore the plain fact that limited resources and space require that someone be charged with the responsibility of picking books to be used in public-school libraries and curriculums. The reality of compulsory schooling, like the reality of television and radio, is that there are a limited number of channels of communication available. The issue in public schools, as in television, comes down to apportioning access to these channels of communication among the contending parties. In school-censorship cases, civil libertarians have asserted the teachers' academic freedom and the students' rights to know, to learn, and to read as limits on school-board power. In contending for this balance of power, however, many civil libertarians have accepted the legitimacy of majority control of socialization in the ordinary operation of schooling. The base line of agreement picked up by the courts in which these parties contest, therefore, is that the school board has the duty and power to control the flow of information and the imposition of beliefs by controlling all aspects of schooling. The question becomes whether there are any circumstances in which the school board can be said to have gone too far in its socializing role.

In an appeals court brief submitted by the New York Civil Liberties Union in the Island Trees censorship case before it went to the Supreme Court, the issue is put this way:

> Though it is plain that traditional First Amendment doctrine prohibits the state from affording greater protection to the views of the majority than the views of the minority, the present controversy is complicated by the fact that it takes place in an institution—the public schools—that has, as one of its recognized goals, the transmittal and perpetuation of societal values. As the District Court noted, a principal function of public education "is indoctrinative, to transmit the basic values of the community." While recognizing the historic inculcative function of public education, the Courts have, nevertheless, been careful to point out that the authority of the state and of school boards, in these respects, is not unlimited.

By "recognizing the historic inculcative function of public education," which is controlled by political majorities, the CLU has substituted a number of lesser questions for the basic question of how a single school system can accommodate the competing desires of families to control how their children are socialized. From the point of view of those who assume the validity of majority controlled socialization, the

CLU position is totally realistic. For others, the contest is over before it begins.

The civil-liberties groups, which take the position that an intelligent balancing of powers among school board, teachers, and students can preserve individual freedom, have placed their hopes in existing community cohesion and in the use of due process and education professionalism in making schooling decisions. They argue not only that each group should have an adequate input into a reasonable decision-making process but that the criteria used by the school board in making decisions about books and curriculum must be reasonable educational criteria. By such an argument, the mere whim or arbitrary personal values of the school board may not be the basis for book removal; and neither may the board remove a book with the intent or effect of imposing a single point of view upon the schools. In its request for the Court to engage in a "concededly delicate" balancing act, the CLU contends that "while school officials can and do foster certain majoritarian values, what they cannot do is to foster majoritarian values by eliminating conflicting values. To do that is to impose a 'pall of orthodoxy.'" In other words, socialization "by persuasion" is permitted while socialization "by coercion" is forbidden. This position is held in spite of the fact that the students' presence in the school is compulsory and their successful completion of the curriculum depends upon their outward agreement with their "persuaders." Even the claim that the school boards' rationale for removing a book must be "compelling" and that the book must be shown to be harmful to students rather than just offensive to majority values, does not make the coercion/persuasion distinction meaningful in public schools.

The CLU and others have thus allowed themselves to be sidetracked onto issues such as due process, reasonable educational criteria, and the meaning of persuasion to a captive audience. The issues are vital to the preservation of some form of dissent in the battle over orthodoxy; but only after the premise of majority control is accepted. Having accepted this premise, more second-level issues appear. A distinction, for example, must be made between "censoring" a book and "selecting" a book. The former is alleged to violate the rights of the minority, the latter to be the duty of the majority. In the Warsaw, Indiana, book-burning feud this "crucial" distinction is described in the civil-liberties brief as follows:

> In *selection* situations, the school board is choosing from a universe of potential materials, and both educational and budgetary considerations make it obvious that not all materials can be selected. In *removal* cases, however, it is clear that the members of the school board are targetting particular materials for their wrath . . . because the school board objects to the political, social or religious content of the materials.

This is a classic case of a distinction without a difference, for which lawyers are famous. It is remarkable that so much energy can be put into defining the difference between selection and removal without ever asking if the very idea of an "approved text" for a captive audience might be contrary to the First Amendment.

One of the many formidable roadblocks to applying the First Amendment to majority-controlled schooling has been the difficulty of providing a legally satisfactory definition of public-school orthodoxy. In a number of cases judges have indicated that they want to know exactly what is being forced down students' throats before the law will acknowledge the right of free inquiry, expression, or value formation. In many instances it is possible to identify which values censors seek to impose and which are already contained in the structure and curriculum of public schools; but these beliefs are rarely systematically organized or as easy to identify and articulate as religious dogma. Many of those who struggle over the value content of the public schools act out frustrations by seeking to impose an order that is itself confused and contradictory. Antifeminism, for example, can be seen running through the efforts of many censors, yet proving that these people are seeking to impose a monolithic view of human relationships is extremely difficult, and understanding how these people want to deal with the sea change in gender conceptions and roles is probably impossible.

The matter is made more difficult because the prevailing orthodoxy in most public schools is a negative one. There is order, but there is no community. Many schools are not simply moral vacuums, they are culturally confusing and devoid of significant shared values. Superficial parameters of behavior are imposed by the school bureaucracy in an effort to maintain control, while the possibility of generating real cohesion and meaning for families and teachers is systematically eliminated. For many students, acculturation in public schools is learning to abandon home or subculture values; to relate to others through roles and rules rather than as whole persons and community members; and to deny meanings, feelings, and intellect. When the prevailing orthodoxy consists of learning to be superficial and unresponsive and to live a bureaucratized life without rebelling, it is no wonder that judges ask for, and civil-liberties lawyers cannot really provide, a capsule definition of the dominant ethic of schools or censors. The essence of this chaotic and contradictory context for acculturation is negativism. This is among the most corrosive of all orthodoxies; but the law has yet to recognize its power.

The Civil Liberties Union and others who defend the dignity of the teaching profession and the personal freedom of students to learn and to participate in open inquiry have not been able to make much headway in the courts. The results of cases decided thus far in federal district courts are very mixed, with school boards winning some and teachers or students winning others. The judges in these conflicting decisions have issued equally ringing rulings to justify their positions. In Chelsea, Massachusetts, for example, Judge Joseph Tauro of the federal district court held that the school board of that town could not constitutionally remove a book of high-school writings from a school library simply because

71

they were offended by the language of a poem, "City," in which a girl laments how men look at her on the street.

> There is more at issue than the poem *City*. If this work may be removed by a committee hostile to its language and theme, then the precedent is set for removal of any other work. The prospect of successive school committees "sanitizing" the school library of views divergent from their own is alarming, whether they do it book by book or one page at a time.

Less than two hundred miles away a different federal court decided that one school district in New York City was justified in removing from the school library a book that described the life of people in another school district of the city.

> We find no impingment upon any basic constitutional values . . . evidently some authorized person or body has to make a determination as to what the library collection will be. It is predictable that no matter what choice of books may be made by whatever section of the academy, some other person or group may well dissent. The ensuing shouts of book burning, witch hunting and violation of academic freedom hardly elevate this intramural strife to first amendment constitutional proportions.

The conflicts among these various cases create pressure for the Supreme Court to address the issue of censorship more clearly than it has in the past. But this same variation of lower court results also points to the substantial confusion that exists in the worlds of law and politics about the function of schooling in a democratic society. In early spring of 1982 the Court did hear its first major censorship case, *Pico* v. *Island Trees*.

When the decision was handed down in early summer, the Court displayed the same confusion and uncertainty about schooling and the First Amendment which has ensnared the lower courts, the disputants, and the law in general. By a 5 to 4 decision the *Pico* case was sent back to the district court for a trial; and the justices wrote seven opinions testifying to how little could be agreed upon. Though the opinion is a victory for rationality in its holding that there are *some* limits to school board power over book removal, the Court provides very little guidance for handling these disputes. To make matters worse, the Court sidestepped issues of curriculum control and library book selection and ruled only on removal of school library books. But worst of all is the damage done to the public need to confront and analyze the contradiction between majority control of schools and intellectual freedom. In opinion after opinion, the justices in *Pico* state, though it has no substantial relevance to their decision, that "local school boards must be permitted 'to establish and apply their curriculum in such a way as to transmit community values . . .'" Yet no justice acknowledges the cost that approving this claimed power would have in endless family conflicts over school socialization, in the destruction of the values of the minority in any community, or in draining the vitality of intellectual freedom in the school. The Court's decision in *Pico* is merely an early and confused step in a long overdue effort to make intellectual freedom and public schooling compatible.

As *Pico* demonstrates the traditional concepts of freedom of expression are not easily applicable to public schools, though the First Amendment itself clearly must apply to schools. In spite of the heroic efforts of some civil libertarians, it is doubtful that these traditional concepts can be made applicable. What is more important is that this effort obscures a more basic issue about schooling—the contradiction between majority control and the First Amendment rights of the minority. School boards that claim absolute power over their captive charges do so in the name of the mythical community majority, thus ignoring the rights of families in the minority to influence school socialization. Civil libertarians have defended the right of some individuals to be free of "the pall of orthodoxy" without being able to take account of the right of other individuals to control the socialization of their children in schools. Both these adversaries ignore the rights of families to hold differing values *and* to have them become part of the unavoidable inculcating process of schooling.

In essence, the concepts used by these parties have allowed them to avoid completely the significance of pitched inter-group conflict over texts and curriculum. Because the emotional, personal, and cultural reality of these conflicts is not taken into account, the solutions advanced do not hold the promise of abating these conflicts. Unless the fundamental importance of voluntary family choice is recognized in the debate over control of compulsory schooling, the war over orthodoxy in these schools is likely to continue its destructive effect on teachers, students, families, board members, and political dissent in American society.

The lessons to be learned from the continuing war over orthodoxy in public schools are distressing:

• The explanations provided by American culture for present reality and the expectations for future behavior in that culture seem less and less valid to the public, and there is, therefore, an increasing sense of confusion and alienation among people concerned with raising children.

• Censorship of books and curriculum in the public schools is a symptom of this collapse of cultural explanations.

• The attempt to require consensus on all issues of conscience and culture in schooling breeds public strife; causes distrust among parents, teachers and students; immobilizes school governance; and fragments the culture even further.

• Traditional concepts of civil liberty have not been adequate for dealing with conflict over orthodoxy in schools. The discussion of *access* to the public school as a value inculcator has been substituted for a discussion of *voluntarism* and family choice of schools.

• The majoritarian structure of schooling, by requiring the attempt at coercive consensus, inevitably violates freedom of belief and expression; but the combatants in these conflicts have refused to recognize this contradiction.

II
DECLARATIONS
OF INDEPENDENCE

. . . conflict seemed to rise irresistibly from deep-lying sources.

How profound the disorder, how fundamental the malaise, is perhaps best indicated by the speed with which humble, crude disputes—disputes of the crassest, least principled character—skidded off their original tracks onto elevating planes of disputation and ended deadlocked in the realm of principle.

—Bernard Bailyn *Origins of American Politics*

Few people can avoid participating in or feeling the results of censorship conflict when it occurs in their school district. Some of those who have the personal or financial resources to escape the war over orthodoxy in public schools choose to educate their children at home. Part Two deals with the experiences of these people. Chapter 7 tells the story of one economically poor but intellectually wealthy family that had to fight for two years to secure the right of home education. Chapters 8, 9, 10 and 11 generalize this family's experience, describing a pattern of anti-institutional dissent and its consequences drawn from the struggles of numerous other families across the country. In Chapter 12, the judiciary's attempt to understand and resolve these conflicts is described, and we see why the conflicts seem destined to continue.

7

Is Educating Your Own Child a Crime?

During the summer of 1977, Peter and Susan Perchemlides planned a home-instruction curriculum for their eight-year-old son, Richard. There was nothing unusual or difficult for them in this task, for these well-educated parents had taught their two oldest sons at home some years earlier. In early September of that year, the plan for Richard's home instruction was submitted for approval to the local superintendent of schools as required by state law. Eight months later, on April 6, 1978, complaints were issued in the District court of Hampshire County in western Massachusetts against the Perchemlideses for failure to send Richard to school. Dr. Perchemlides, who has a Ph.D. in biochemistry, had been accused of the crime of educating his own son.

The Perchemlideses came to the Amherst area in 1975, drawn by the quiet beauty of the rolling hills and small farms spreading east from the Connecticut River. In their view, the academic institutions that set the tone for the area—the University of Massachusetts, Amherst, Hampshire College, Smith, and Mt. Holyoke—and the tolerant and progressive reputation of the schools and families in town would all contribute to the health and development of the family. This move was a substantial change from life in Boston where Peter had been first a research fellow at the Massachusetts General Hospital and later a research associate at the Harvard University Medical School. Upon arrival in Amherst, Richard was enrolled in the second grade at a local elementary school, Mark's Meadow, run in conjunction with the University of Massachusetts' School of Education. The two oldest of the family's five children were enrolled in the public-school system as well, and everything seemed promising.

After a year and a half, the promise turned sour, and home education seemed the only reasonable response. Peter Perchemlides had been trying for eighteen months to influence Richard's public-school education. By serving on numerous public-school planning committees, he believes he saw the predominant values in the hidden curriculum of the Amherst public schools: conformity, anti-intellectualism, passivity, alienation, classism, and hierarchy. His struggle to reverse these values has taught him a lesson he had not expected.

In Susan Perchemlides's view, the public schools "break down and categorize curriculum, and they break down and categorize children too." It is tracking in disguise, a means of defining a child in a limited sphere and then working to internalize that image in the child's mind. After a few months at Mark's Meadow, Susan says, "Richard seemed to lose his openness and ease with adults and older children and retreat to shyness." She attributes this development not only to fear but also to the imposition of the idea that a seven-year-old "is supposed to be into TV and games and not aware of the world around him, that he is most comfortable with kids his own age and has a developing consumer consciousness." Here is how Richard put the matter in an affidavit submitted to the court in mid-September:

> I was embarrassed at school—at first because it was new but later because I was laughed at. I was at a beginning

level in some things, and they didn't understand why. It made it hard for me to do the work even if I wanted to.

I like it better here, at home. My parents teach me some things that are really different. We do music, art, math, cooking, earth sciences, gardening, ecology, astronomy, reading, writing, spelling, and yoga. Reading is different from how it was at school. I'm reading some now—books that are more interesting . . . like *A Cranberry Thanksgiving*. I'm not embarrassed, and I like to check out the other kids on the stuff I'm learning—they don't know it. Some of them called me dumb because I don't go to their school, but they found out I was learning a lot. Most of the kids think I'm lucky.

Forty-two and balding, his face framed by a full, dark beard lined with traces of gray, Peter thinks the problem of "fit," of conformity, was the central issue in 1978: "The school looks for behavioral patterns in kids, and when the kid departs from what they expect and see the majority doing, then this represents to them some kind of problem, and their function then is to identify the problem and develop a program to deal with it." Richard's individuality and his family's individual values became a handicap, rather than a strength in this setting.

The family sees anti-intellectuality in the "school's failure to come to grips with differing and critical perspectives. The school impresses on kids in subtle ways that they do not have the potential to function in sophisticated ways at diverse things." To the Perchemlideses, schools stress the importance of social skills to the exclusion of any others, so that a child feels he must search for a role in life. This, they believe, is reinforced by the child's seeing that janitors, students, teachers, administrators are arranged in a hierarchy of importance. The child becomes preoccupied with "Where in this hierarchy do I fit?" Passive acceptance of the existing order and an inability to think outside of self-interest result.

Susan, a strong, blonde woman with an intellectual tone to her criticisms, does not like the school's attitude that home education would be "confusing" to the child by teaching him on a less simplistic level than he receives at school. Raised in Appalachia, she says she is insulted by the school's undercutting of the family's class-consciousness, its views on social justice, and its values about the relationship of man and nature.

Looking back over the first year of what was to become a seemingly interminable controversy, Richard, at nine and a half, recalled his reactions to the one year he spent in the public school: "If you did something wrong, everyone would laugh. You had to do it just so, and it was boring to do it that way." Perhaps this is the meaning of the story Susan tells about Richard's reaction at school when asked to provide a caption for a drawing of a woman in fancy clothes waving at someone. Richard reportedly thought it was "a working-class woman all dressed up to go somewhere she didn't get to go much," but was afraid that if he said this the school counselor "wouldn't like us and our family." He simply replied, "I don't know."

When a home-education plan was drafted by the Perchemlideses, it was based not only on their earlier experiences in educating the older boys at home but also on their own views of natural and social order and on their reaction against the values, philosophy, and practices of the Amherst School Department. The curriculum document itself is extensive, containing page after page of detailed plans in such areas as language arts, earth science, ecology, music, mathematics, nutrition and health, and physical education, including a two-mile jog each day. The document has been reviewed by numerous education experts and found to be sound. Dr. David Campbell of the University of Pittsburgh School of Education, a consultant to public and private schools on curriculum and methodology and the author of several books and over forty articles, found the Perchemlideses' program to be "the equivalent of a first-rate private academy both in its tutorial system and in . . . the curriculum."

When the family first raised the issue of home instruction with the Amherst Superintendent of Schools, Donald Frizzle, it apparently caught him by surprise. When asked later what his initial reaction had been, he commented, "I'd never been asked that before, and I had no particular procedures that I would normally just follow." Frizzle gave the family a form ordinarily used by the school department for private-school approvals and told them to do the best they could with it. Meanwhile, he began a search for clarification of his legal powers and duties. Massachusetts compulsory attendance law requires that every child between the ages of six and sixteen attend a public school or a private school approved by the local public-school board or be "otherwise instructed in a manner approved in advance by the local superintendent or school committee." The problem was not only that there were no prepared forms and procedures for the approval of home education plans but that neither Frizzle nor the school committee had standards for making such approvals.

The Perchemlideses claimed no religious basis for their convictions about family values and the meaning of life. They were conscientious objectors without religious identification. The family sought to comply with that part of Massachusetts law that makes home instruction a right after approval by the local school superintendent.

The crucial issue on this point is whether the government may so regulate a legislatively sanctioned alternative to public schooling that its distinctive quality is eliminated or contorted. In spite of the negative view that both court and Constitution have taken in the past toward government monopoly on education, the desire to hang on to power seems to have prompted the Amherst school authorities to claim "absolute discretion" in passing judgment upon home education plans and to dismiss the parents' plan and values as "pet educational theories."

Confronted with a unique local case, Superintendent Frizzle and his staff were genuinely confused about how to react. Perhaps it was beyond their experience to be confronted with a family that insisted on defining what was best for their child's education. But the kind of process that the school department established to deal with this situation is an indication that they perceived a threat to professional power and government control of education in the Perchemlideses' request. From interviews, depositions, and internal memoranda, the picture that emerges is one of school authorities trying to avoid a head-on conflict.

At the outset the superintendent asked for the submission of a written home-education plan but did not outline any standards the parents would be required to meet. Considering that failure to meet the school department's criteria could expose the family to criminal sanctions and even, ultimately, to the seizure of their son by the state Welfare Department, this vagueness would itself be enough to merit legal condemnation as a denial of due process. Upon submission the plan was turned over to the school-department staff for evaluation. Later, the superintendent was to claim that the standards of judgment were those mentioned in the statute for the approval of private schools, namely, that the program "equals in thoroughness and efficiency, and in the progress made therein, that in the public schools in the same town." Just what this equivalence really meant was not specified, but counsel for the family, Wendy Sibbison, knew it could not literally mean "the same as" the public schools or a whole string of cases would have to be overruled.

The school department offered a four-inch-thick sheaf of papers purporting to describe the curriculum of the school system. Did the parents have to make their plan equal to that? Frizzle replied, "The burden is on the person who wants to do this." But did the parents have to equal every detail of the curriculum? No, but the parents could not be told which aspects they had to match "because that would be an invasion of their values and policy." They must "do what they feel is proper"; then judgment would be passed.

As it turned out, that judgment was passed on the proposed program on October 7, 1977, when the Perchemlideses were notified that their plan had been rejected. Although each of the four grounds on which the plan was denied was based on lack of information, the family was not asked for further details. Neither was the family ever confronted with the negative opinions of the school department's experts or given a chance to refute or counter them prior to the decision.

The reasons themselves are part of the roller coaster of confusion created by the school department. Although the plan is for *home* instruction, the superintendent disapproved of the plan in part because it provided no "group experiences." The school department was unaware that a 1967 New Jersey case, *N.J.* v. *Massa*, dealt with just this issue, ruling that "to hold that the statute requires equivalent social contact and development would emasculate this alternative and allow only group education, thereby eliminating private tutoring for home education."

The superintendent also objected that the family had made no indication that they had the "training or background appropriate to the task you propose to undertake." Although Frizzle publicly admitted his respect for the family's home life and for Peter's "immense intelligence" and "deep philosophical thinking," he noted that a Ph.D. does not necessarily know how to teach children. Yet the family had educated the two oldest sons, Greg and Steven, at home for four years; they were then enrolled in Amherst public schools where they received As and Bs their first year.

After their plan was rejected, the family sought a review of the case before the school committee, whose power is concurrent with that of the superintendent. Here the standards become still more confusing and contradictory, and the procedure becomes still more Orwellian.

The school committee met five times to discuss the case. At the first meeting, the family was present with counsel, but no hearing was held because the school committee found it necessary to request additional curriculum information from the Perchemlideses and to seek legal counsel on their powers in this matter. The committee subsequently received both sets of information but never notified the parents or their attorneys of the meetings at which all the facts were to be considered, the expert opinions heard, and the witnesses examined.

Considering that the parents might still have suffered criminal penalties and lost their son to the state, proceedings before the school committee resembled the Star Chamber. The family had no notice of hearing; no counsel present; no opportunity to present its own expert witnesses about the quality or philosophy of the curriculum they proposed; no opportunity to cross-examine or even hear the witnesses who testified their plan was unacceptable; no knowledge of the standards being applied; and, ultimately, no statement of the reasons for the school committee's December 16, 1977, denial of their request.

During all this time, the Perchemlideses continued to educate Richard at home, trying to undo what they viewed as the damage done by Richard's year in the Amherst public school. Richard, like the rest of the family, was under intense and increasing pressure as a result of the conflict with the school authorities. After a year in the spotlight, Richard would admit that he "liked being recognized." "But," he was quick to add, "I like even better just staying at home."

After the school committee's denial of the family's "appeal" and its refusal on January 30, 1978, to reconsider, the school department began to increase the pressure on the family. Up to that point, the superintendent had seen no need to "jam the law on them" and had never really questioned the sincerity of their teaching efforts or the adequacy of their home environment. In fact, in a deposition given during the summer of 1978, Frizzle admitted that he had implicitly approved the home instruction plan earlier.

Between threats, negotiations, and a general reluctance to set the wheels of the criminal law in motion, it was not until April 16, 1978, that criminal charges were finally brought against the Perchemlideses under the state truancy statute. The family's lawyers, working virtually without pay because Peter was unemployed and Susan was a full-time student, immediately filed a civil suit seeking to halt the criminal

84

prosecution, to force the school authorities to formulate standards for approval of home-education plans, and to approve the family's plan pursuant to such standards.

The family's suit contended that the school committee's standards for approval of home education must be minimal. Since the family's rights of privacy, conscience, and belief are at risk in government regulation of education, the suit sought to require that any regulation of the right of home education in Massachusetts be justified by a compelling state interest. Most importantly, the Perchemlideses called for an end to the practice by which education standards and truancy laws are used to impose the educational philosophy and political and cultural values of the school bureaucracy upon individual families.

The school authorities sought to prevent a public hearing of the facts before the superior court by taking the position that the parents had no claim and should therefore be dismissed from the court. The criminal charges were dismissed because of the pending civil suit, but they hung like a cloud over the family because they could be renewed if the family were unsuccessful at trial.

It is ironic that this case should have developed in the Commonwealth of Massachusetts, which considers itself the birthplace of universal education and the cradle of individual liberty in America. As the case moved beyond the personal struggle of one family and one school bureaucracy, it seemed increasingly to bring into question whether something had happened in the development of public education to have brought it into conflict with the principles of individual liberty and free and vigorous dissent upon which our constitutional order rests. One might have thought that this contradiction was put to rest in 1925 when the *Pierce* case denied the legitimacy of a government monopoly of schooling. One might also have thought the matter had been settled in Massachusetts in 1897 when the state's highest court interpreted the compulsory education statute to allow home education and enunciated the purpose of compulsory education to be "that all children shall be educated, not that they shall be educated in any particular way." But the issue refused to go away.

On September 13, 1978, Judge John Greaney of the Hampshire County Superior Court handed down his opinion in the case of *Perchemlides* v. *Frizzle,* finding that the family had "not received all the process that was due them" from the school committee and that the rejection of the home-education plan "may have occurred for reasons that were impermissible on the state of the law." The case was returned to the school committee with instructions to reassess the plan in accordance with the requirements of due process and in the absence of impermissible criteria such as "the parents' reasons for wanting to educate their child at home; the lack of a curriculum identical to that provided in the public schools; and the lack of group experience." But Judge Greaney's learned review of Massachusetts law and the provisions of the federal Constitution left the school department free to make its determination on the basis of such standards as "the manner in which the subjects are taught so as to impart comparable knowledge as given in the local schools; . . . and the adequacy of texts, materials, methods, and programs being used." The great gray area in which the discretion of public-school officials can become a source for official disapproval of dissenting values was not much constricted by this decision.

Following the decision, which was widely interpreted as a victory for the family, negotiations produced an approval of the Perchemlideses' home-education plan, provided that it was accompanied by an evaluation system monitored by a neutral third party. Richard remained at home, being educated as his parents desired, but uncertainty also remained in the Perchemlideses' home. They did not know whether they might, at some future time, overstep the vague boundaries of proper education as defined by public-school officials.

8
A Hostile Environment for Individualism

As the Perchemlides case shows, the handful of families who choose to avoid institutionalized schooling in favor of home-based learning have set off a storm of professional hostility. The wreckage caused by the storm often includes the altered lives of ordinary American families, public doubt about the adequacy of official views of education, and a warning that the ideology of schooling has become brittle and contradictory.

Home schooling is as much a rarity today as it was a commonplace in Colonial America. Where home schooling was once accepted and considered natural, it has since become the object of suspicion and defensiveness. Where it once expressed the central social importance of family, it is now viewed as an expression of idiosyncrasy and antisocial sentiment. What once demonstrated the personal and life-related nature of learning is now seen as a threat to the smooth operation of the nation's most pervasive bureaucracy. The symbolic significance of home education has increased as its practice and real importance to the school systems in which it arises have decreased.

The fact that there are so very few twentieth-century

American families educating their children at home might be understood as an indication that "unschooling," as some call it, is a nonissue in a society of mass institutions. But these families have touched a raw nerve in American society, and the reaction to them points to substantial ideological contradictions in local schooling and national culture.

The formal, institutional school has become America's most common cultural experience and its biggest business. It is hardly surprising that we have all but abandoned the urge to participate in the education of children in favor of the ease of institutional schooling. To do otherwise would be impractical and inconsistent with our lifestyle. The tasks of getting a job and putting food on the table and of keeping up payments on the American dream require so much time and energy that often only the day's dregs are left for the cultivation of family and the education of children.

If a child is in school six hours each day for twelve years merely as a logical result of changes in the social and economic structure over the last 200 years, why do a few thousand families seeking to educate their children at home evoke such virulent official reactions and such widespread public attention? Why is it that millions of children who are pushouts or dropouts amount to business as usual in the public schools, while one family educating a child at home becomes a major threat to universal public education and the survival of democracy?

Even a brief listing of the consequences endured by those who seek official approval for home education is startling. In Iowa parents who educate their nine-year-old son at home are convicted of criminal violations. They appeal, are acquitted, and are threatened with renewed prosecution the next year. In Michigan a family is forced to send three of their children to a boarding school 150 miles from home to avoid the threat of having their children made wards of the court and sent to foster homes. In Massachusetts a family is accused of parental neglect for educating two teenagers at home, and the children are removed to the custody of the welfare department. After a long struggle, the family is split up and scattered over three states. Another family is told by a judge to comply with school requirements or move out of the state. In Rhode Island a couple is arrested for educating their daughters, aged eight and nine, at home. In Missouri a woman spends time behind bars because she does not believe her seven-year-old is ready for school.

In none of these cases did anyone seriously question the health or happiness of the children or suggest they were being abused or neglected in any way other than in their parents' failure to send them to schools most people attend. What accounts for the failure to compromise these conflicts before such heavy-handed tactics are brought to bear? Why do public officials apparently feel driven to behave as if they were fighting a dread disease rather than disagreeing with a solitary dissenter?

To some extent, of course, the media makes the message. The single eccentric family articulating its differences with school ideology by a publicly proclaimed act of civil disobedience makes much more interesting reading or viewing than a mass of silent dissenters whose only articulation of their alienation from institutional education is to hang out on street corners. In the past two years every major news magazine, network television magazine, and talk show has done a human-interest story on home education. The national meetings of state education superintendents and other professional educators have found themselves discussing the "issue" of home schooling as if it amounted to a national movement to abolish schooling. Newsletters circulate among practicing and would-be "unschoolers," legal defense networks are organized, regional meetings are held among parents. There is a sense that a family's commitment to solitary home schooling is an expression of some of the deepest resentments toward the most bottled up hopes for American society. The attractiveness of the continuing conflict over home education as a media event, the excessive reactions it evokes from school authorities, and the symbolic importance it has for the participants are all based on the cultural dislocations the conflict reveals.

School conflict is a microcosm of social stress because schooling is accessible politics. Conflict over schooling is visible, local, and more nearly legible than any other aspect of public-policy debate. Not only does every community have a school and a ponderous school budget but every adult feels entitled to demand that the schools serve his or her own interests. The issues of school policy seem mundane—what texts should be required, how much discipline or competitiveness is appropriate, how should science be taught, what method of reading instruction works best—but individuals often project onto the screen of public-school policy their deepest feelings about how society ought to be structured and how children ought to be socialized into that society. For most people, schooling is the only game in town; and so it is in the debate over school policy that basic cultural and personal values enter the public arena. On this ground of accessible and pervasive politics, the conflict over home schooling can become a symbolic struggle over the creation of public orthodoxy and the preservation of individual idiosyncrasy. It is a struggle in which we may read cultural meanings from apparently personal texts.

In spite of the diversity of families seeking to educate their children at home and in spite of the localism of schools opposing those families, there is a typical pattern of events and a commonality of themes in the conflict over unschooling. In fact, during the past two years of talking with families, school superintendents, lawyers, state school officials, and others about home education, I have seen the myriad cases blend into one and the dozens of personal aspirations and institutional responses form a single predictable course of events. Not all the conflicts run the full course, but wherever they drop off, all are following the same general path.

Many observers agree with John Holt's guess that upwards of ten thousand American families educate their children at home, but there are indications that under this accessible surface, a much larger number of families educate their children at home without requesting approval. And it must be recognized that a few families gain the support and approval of local school officials without a struggle, thereby proving that private aspirations are not necessarily a threat to public welfare. This section concerns those dissenting families who do find themselves in conflict with school authorities over home education. Since this conflict is symptomatic of larger issues, my aim is to show what can be learned from these conflicts about the function of schooling and the form of dissent in a society dependent on large institutions for child rearing.

The unfolding of home-schooling conflict must begin with the family decision against schooling, proceed through the search for approval of school authorities, examine the reaction of the community, and conclude with the formal proceedings in courts of law. As the pattern unfolds, individuals become actors in a play based on a script they did not write. The struggle becomes one of high-magnitude social and schooling problems that overshadow the needs and preferences of the participants. Even before the court hearing, there is evidence that important social issues hover just beneath the surface of personal decisions and professional postures. The story of home-schooling conflicts is the story of the emergence of basic social issues and their eventual domination of the meaning and action of individual disputes.

Of the many problems that emerge during the two or three years of a typical confrontation over home instruction, none seems more basic and intractable than the cultural contradiction between individualism and institutional life. It is a contradiction that has not been caused by the 100-year evolution of institutional schooling in America but whose poignancy is greatly exaggerated by that schooling. It is in the schooling of young minds that the culture requires the simultaneous absorption of both the ideology of individual dignity and the practice of institutional conformity. Few of the participants ever become aware of the significance their struggle holds for culture-wide issues of this magnitude.

91

9
Adaptation and Change

The family that chooses to teach its children at home is a kind of social mutant. It exhibits behavior altered in one detail from the common pattern of family life; and the problem created thereby is whether this mutation will make the family more or less adaptive and likely to survive. These families will be treated as a composite unit: the dissenting family, whose struggle for survival is intensified by the home-schooling decision. By not sending their children to school, the dissenting family has abandoned a habit of life that has seemed adaptive for generations. In most cases the parents attended public school themselves in the fifties and have survived; and so did their parents before them. It is difficult to say exactly why this mutation is manifesting itself now rather than at an earlier time, but a very small percentage of Americans have come to view their family's survival as linked more to home education than to institutional schooling.

Family decisions against institutional schooling range from the impulsive to the ideologically sophisticated. For some parents the decision not to send a child to school is not thought out at all. They are simply pursuing life as usual. According to one mother, "Everyone else just stopped teaching their children when they were six, and we just kept on going." There is no belief that any special effort or sudden change in life is called for merely because it happens to be the first September after a child's sixth birthday. In the future, they acknowledge, they may feel a sense of inadequacy in some areas of child rearing. But for now, the legal line of demarcation embodied in a compulsory school attendance statute seems arbitrary—designed for a hypothetical child in a hypothetical family.

To another mother, the problem was no more complex, the response no more planned out: "In the second week of first grade, I was walking Heidi out to wait with her for the school bus and she asked me why she had to go to school. I couldn't think of a single reason that I really agreed with. We just turned right around and came back home, and that was it." Helping her child to learn letters, the sounds they stand for, and the words they make didn't seem like intimidating tasks to this mother. What the school could do, the family could do as well. To suddenly give up part of your role as a parent in favor of an "expert" would require some good reasons. Heidi had asked what those reasons might be, but the ideology that would have provided the right answers, the quick answers, just wasn't in her mother's grasp. She herself had been unhappy in the California public schools and wasn't particularly well educated in spite of her intelligence and her regular attendance.

Neither of these parents considered whether the upcoming conflict would be worth the trouble compared to the benefits of schooling already paid for from taxes. In fact, no conflict was anticipated at all. The habit was for the child to be at home with the parents. Breaking this habit and taking up the more popular one of attendance just didn't seem right. There was an unarticulated feeling that the child belonged at home and not in an institution. For some, especially single mothers, home teaching is an adequate compromise between the traditional role of motherhood and the desire to do nondomestic work.

Some families are more conscious of the importance of their decision. They have a preconceived idea of education, which helps them resist the force exerted by the doctrine of attendance and makes the entire process of home education more self-conscious. An Iowa professor and his wife reflected on their own experiences and on some readings they have collected from libertarian literature:

> Classrooms are confined spaces in which students read *about* the rest of the world . . . , but are carefully kept from it, where they do not have to be taken seriously. We feel we can and do eliminate this artificial barrier between education and life . . . by educating our child at home.

Fully developed, this ideology holds not only that school separates learning from life but that inside the institution of school, fragmentation and alienation are reproduced in curriculum, programmed bits of knowledge, graded progress, and measured results.

This same conception of schooling—that classrooms and a formal curriculum warp and diminish learning—also appears as a ready explanation for the change in a child's demeanor perceived by the parents after a year or two of schooling. Some parents remove their children from school because they have observed their natural curiosity and eagerness becoming dulled by age eight or nine: "I remember my children being very intuitive, curious, . . . they seemed to have a natural, inner motivation that led them from experience to experience, . . . their delicate minds were left alone, unpressured . . . We have noticed a gradual loss of interest, and we've become concerned that our children are being drained of their ability to learn since they began school. What has happened to the zest they once possessed?" These parents, a thirteen-year veteran of a local police force and a certified schoolteacher, found their children unwilling to share their school experience with them, as if they were

self-conscious about their struggles in school or bent on pre-
serving the privacy of a new life apart from the family.
School was seen as a threat to family relations.

Yet even children who were communicative about their
school experiences provided their parents with support for a
nascent antischool ideology that holds that mastering the
bureaucratic path of programmed steps and units is a substitute for natural curiosity and real necessity in learning. In
one family, anger and sadness resulted when a father failed
to recognize that his daughter was proud not of having mas-
tered a skill in arithmetic but of having advanced from one
level to another. The kind of communication and behavior
required at school was making communication and learning
harder at home.

At times, the hostility toward the fragmentation and
bureaucratization of knowledge that justifies some home-
schooling decisions can resemble a reaction against all outside sources of learning. In the voices of some dissenting
families you can hear an antisocial epistemology: "How can
our children ever find this 'teacher' (Holy Spirit) within if
they are instilled with the idea that schools, classrooms,
textbooks, and human beings are the sources of knowledge?" Is this a denial of human responsibility and a fragment of religious fundamentalism, the dry seed of an old-
time religion? Is it the "holy curiosity of learning," of which
Einstein spoke in his opposition to compulsory learning? Or
is it a call for deschooling society and for curbing self-serving
institutions? For many religious families, the "teacher
within" provides some rationalization for the resistance to
schooling.

The fragments of antischool thinking with which some
families arm themselves are on occasion part of a general
antistate or antiauthoritarian sentiment. Sometimes the families are barely conscious of these beliefs at the time a child is
taken out of school but on reexamination the beliefs are seen
to be more than mere coincidences in the life of the family.

Peter Perchemlides was articulate in his opposition to
schooling for his sons and in his ability to identify the values

advanced by the local public school. But his anti-authoritarianism did not emerge fully until after the school conflict began. In general, he does not believe that the state—the political majority—has a legitimate interest in how his sons are educated or what they come to believe. He remembers stories from his own parents about the power of the state and the consequences for those who dissent from the dominant ethic of society.

When Peter's Greek grandfather was a middle-aged man, he lived in what is now Turkey. He was shot and killed by agents of the state for refusing conscription into an armed force that was to fight against the Greeks. Peter's father was fourteen at the time and managed to escape and came eventually to America, where Peter was born in 1937. The story did not have much of a conscious impact on Peter until the sixties, when the issues of conscription, war, and the power of the state became loudly public and personally painful. Peter's skepticism about government power grew. Later, when he became involved in a pitched battle with the Amherst, Massachusetts, school authorities, he never could be convinced that the state's interest in the family's education plans amounted to anything less than the psychological conscription of young minds. Peter was not killed for his resistance to this conscription; but it did cost over four thousand dollars and two years of family anguish and constant struggle before a court told the local school board that the family had a constitutional right to home education for their sons.

A substantial number of dissenting families have developed just such comprehensive opinions about the limits of government and about the legitimate interests of the state in controlling knowledge, attitudes, and beliefs in the young. In fact, home-schooling families are forced to articulate their views and clarify their values by the conflicts in which they become involved. As a result of these conflicts, most of these parents eventually look back to their own experiences in the public schools, back to themselves as young adults in the sixties and seventies, and even back to their more distant family histories for the source of their resistance to schooling. In talking about the general exercise of state power over what they view as personal and private family decisions, there is an acknowledgment that the public has an interest in being sure that every child is educated. But the public, they believe, has no business deciding *how* the child shall be educated. Actions of the state against dissenting families are contributing to the spread of antistate ideology.

The opposition of families to public prescription of what shall be learned is most fully articulated among those families who see the struggle as one against a dysfunctional ideology they believe is foisted upon children by their school system. These families are fully conscious of the fact that they dissent from widely accepted values and beliefs. There is great variation in the values held by these families and in their predictions about what the world will be like when their children grow up. They do not agree with each other about what skills and attitudes will best insure the survival of parent and child. Their politics range the spectrum from far right to left and from religious fundamentalism to secular agnosticism; but they all are convinced that the attitudes and beliefs underlying public schools are wrong for their families and will make their children's survival more, rather than less, difficult.

These families can point to experiences of unwanted values in school that include a wide range of required behaviors, prohibited expressions, confessions of belief, restrictions of knowledge in curriculum, didactic statements, and role models. The interrelationship between belief and behavior is complex for children just learning to understand their world; and parents make no distinctions about whether it is the belief or the behavior that seems more harmful. If a teacher constantly behaves as if boys were supposed to be restricted to mechanical skills and aggressive roles while girls are supposed to concern themselves politely with domestic and artistic endeavors, that seems no less threatening than if the teacher made everyone recite "What Are Little Girls Made Of?" The recitation of the pledge of allegiance is no less offensive to the parent opposed to idolatry and

97

chauvinism than shaming a child for making a mistake in class is to the parent who feels competitive attitudes are harmful and dysfunctional. As a practice offensive to families, it is hard to distinguish authoritarianism in the operation of the classroom from the preaching of authoritarianism in a social-studies lesson.

Anyone who has studied a child's textbook or observed the daily routine of schooling knows there is more to schooling than what is stated in the curriculum. The making of curricular choices, the need for order in the classroom, and the bureaucratic needs of school systems all require that children be encouraged, cajoled, and coerced into compliance with school and classroom structure. The conformity with school structure, which children must express in order to succeed in school, is a confession of belief in the values underlying the structure. Even dissenting parents who do not view school indoctrination as effective are deeply offended when their children act as if school values really define right and wrong.

The description of families seeking home education for their children has been centered on the attitudes and beliefs of parents. Most of the children of these families were under the age of twelve, and none of them evidenced anything but support for the decision their parents had made. In most instances the children appeared to have been allowed at least a limited part in the family's decision-making process and could articulate their desires for home education without sounding as if they had been coached excessively. It is not difficult to imagine, however, that there are families in which the children dissent from the parents' decision to stay home, just as there are children who resist receiving their schooling in an institution. And there must be children who do not accept the substance of what their parents seek to indoctrinate in them.

To explore the complexities of the relationship between child and parent in home schooling; to plumb the psychology of rebellion, coercion, growth, and autonomy within these families; to relate these family patterns to a pragmatic theory of children's rights and the role of family in society would require another research project altogether. It will have to suffice here to observe that the rights of children in families will probably be easier to understand and protect once the consequences of overbearing state pressures on the families themselves have been articulated.

There is a temptation on the part of people who feel the times are sadly out of joint to see any of the families that object to schooling as either heroic champions of a new humanism or as fanatically misguided adherents of old and worn dogmas. In reality these dissenting families seem much more modest. They are simply trying to survive by adopting values that make sense to them and fit with their understanding of society, with their vision—however blurred—of what the future holds. Like mutants of other species, history may judge these organisms to have made the wrong change, to have arrived in a cultural cul-de-sac. If so, it will be because they have become misfits, failures, creatures without a socio-ecological niche. But it is also possible that they will survive as families and as people and that it is the rest of us who are taking the wrong fork in the social road. In either case, dissenting families doubt that majority approval makes the attitudes and beliefs of a school system useful or adaptive for the future. For each family the struggle against a particular dysfunctional ideology is also the struggle against the idea that one family or group should prescribe for another what all are in such doubt about.

As the struggles proceed, each family expresses its own values more and more through opposition to the school system. Statements about the positive beliefs of the family become mixed with negative statements about the schools. The conflict over whose values shall be empowered and therefore prevail combined with the extreme difficulty of becoming aware of the values that really operate in one's life make this negativism almost inevitable.

The primary value shared by the antischool families is, of course, the belief that their children will be better educated within the fabric of the family and away from the institutional requirements of any school. For some, it might have been possible to find a private school that did reflect family values. But this was not acceptable, either because the private school was too expensive for a family already supporting one school system with its tax dollars or because the family opposed institutionalized schooling of any kind. In addition, many dissenting families resist the private-school alternative as long as possible because the values the family seeks to maintain, nurture, or create are not to be found in any available school, public or private. Because their dissent is so individualistic, there is no subculture or institution with which they can identify.

It is impossible to do justice to all the different attitudes and world views held by the families who resist schooling. The variety of these views is testament to the individualism of the families, and the story of their conflict with school authorities concerns the consequences of individual dissent rather than the merits or popularity of their views.

It is possible, though, to assemble a rough catalogue of some of their criticisms of the school systems—of the ideology they find dysfunctional. To many of the families of children schooled at home, the values in which public school students must confess belief include the following:

1. Authority in society should be organized hierarchically, and it is appropriate for those of less authority to cultivate attributes of obedience and passivity.

2. Truth is prescribed and established by authority and learning means understanding and accepting the official version of reality.

3. Material acquisition, rather than spiritual condition, is the most significant measure of personal success and social progress; and measurement, rather than intuition, defines knowledge.

4. Competition is more important than cooperation.

5. The ability to follow directions is more important than creativity, and dissent is either the result of poor communication, willful misanthropy, or emotional instability.

100

No single family articulates the values underlying public schooling in just this language; and all the families offended by beliefs they see enshrined in public schools do not agree on which values constitute public orthodoxy. The list of offensive school beliefs grows, however, with each conversation one has with "unschoolers."

6. Poverty, malnutrition, disease, oppression, and violence are not created by anyone who lives according to society's rules, and people in general should perform whatever acts are required by their "roles" without ethical discomfort.

7. Compulsion and coercion are acceptable means of creating proper behavior, including learning.

8. There are specific character attributes associated with race, gender, class, and age that cannot be changed and upon which may be based the distribution of power, wealth, and dignity.

9. Institutional schooling contributes to the progress of the individual and society, upgrades general morality, reduces prejudice, and protects each rising generation from the mistakes of the previous generation.

10. Manual labor can never attain the dignity or power of intellectual labor; and art, music and mysticism are nonessential.

As the list of criticisms of public-school values grows, one becomes aware that the perceived orthodoxy these families oppose is characteristic not simply of schools but of the culture in general. The fact that the development of their children's consciences is at stake and that compulsory schooling is a major part of child rearing provides an opportunity for social criticism. It is the transmission of culture that is at stake for these dissenters.

The list of values that home-school advocates object to in public and private schooling is virtually endless and frequently contradictory because the values by which these parents judge schools are so varying and multitudinous. Although their conflicts over home schooling have pushed these parents toward clarity, none have developed a com-

101

plete statement of their own beliefs and world views or of the ways in which these beliefs are thwarted by the schools.

Most historians of education and observers of present-day schooling have tried to discern the central values expressed by schools and to show with which interest group or political decision these values are associated. It may indeed be possible to describe the dominant values of a school or of schooling in general at any particular point in time and space. But the families who have chosen to educate their children at home do not feel the need for such scholarly explication of the basic facts they sense from their own experience. Whatever their particular beliefs or world views, these parents and the scholars whose work they sometimes find helpful agree, as Jonathan Kozol has put it, that "the containment of youth, which lies at the heart of school indoctrination, depends upon the demolition of a child's ideological and ethical perceptions . . ." Rejecting the notion that any education can be value neutral, dissenting parents want to substitute their own ideology of survival for that which is found in the schools.

As we pass from reflex or habit in family decisions against school attendance to general antischool and antistate ideology and then finally to the particulars of belief and concept a dissenting family finds essential to survival, we are left with a hodgepodge of partially contradictory claims read from between the lines of common questions. Will my children accept inferior social and political roles for women? Will they perceive themselves as dependent upon the group or act on the assumption that their own welfare can be achieved at the expense of others? Will they learn to look down on manual work? Will they become alienated from learning itself as the price of attaining technical certification? What will they learn about the proper relationship of individuals to power and authority; about mysticism, emotion, and art as part of social life; about God, communal living, achievement, violence, personal inadequacy and pleasure; about people's relationship to the natural environment and the manipulation of other human beings?

Whatever their values, these parents recognize that the school is an environment from which a child may learn much more than is in the formal curriculum. They know the effect of the school's molding of children's consciousness is to alter their concept of reality and therefore their perception of and reaction to all things. With some changed perceptions about life and schooling, these families are not waiting to develop a complete self-appraisal before educating their children at home.

10
The Ecology of Bureaucracy:
MEETING WITH SCHOOL AUTHORITIES

In the fall of 1979, an article on the front page of the *New York Times* warned that several hundred species of birds, fish, animals, and plants were in danger of extinction. The reason given was not a shift in ecological conditions but the failure of the Department of the Interior to add these species to its endangered list within the time limit specified by law. On first reading, one might have felt anger at inept bureaucrats and a sense of loss that part of the natural world was about to disappear. But then Darwin's concept of natural selection came reassuringly to mind: Only those adapted to the environment would survive. What these species had failed to adapt to, however, was not so much the natural environment as manmade changes in environment. What was more important was they had not adapted to the ecology of bureaucracy. They could not survive in nature without a bureaucratic category and a timely listing with an unnatural institution.

The families that choose to educate their children at home face this same struggle to fit within a bureaucratically imposed structure in order to survive. In thirty-one of fifty states, this manmade environment consists of compulsory education laws and judicial decisions permitting some form of home education. The specific conditions a family must meet in order to avoid running afoul of the truancy laws vary a great deal among these states. But nearly all require at the very least that a local school superintendent be satisfied that the family's home education plan is "equivalent" to the education offered by the public school.

The elements of this equivalency are extremely vague; and virtually no state except New Hampshire has published a clear and understandable set of standards by which a family could judge whether it qualified for approval. What little case law exists in this area makes it clear that the state may not require that home education be *identical* to the public school program but that the parents may not educate their children at home without some form of accountability to the state. In this extraordinarily vague, discretionary, and often arbitrary setting, the dissenting family must seek the approval of school authorities for home education. The family's failure to fit into this bureaucratic niche will result in the extinction of its home-schooling plan.

The survival of home education in an environment designed for public schools is unlikely, no matter how much lip service that home education might receive or whether it might be the key to survival in the society at large. In fact, survival in a predatory school bureaucracy may be antithetical to survival in society. It is understandable, therefore, that for most school superintendents, it is disorientating to be approached by a family that does not want to send its child to the public school and believes it can provide a better than adequate education at home. The vagueness of the statutes and the absence of past experience with home-schooling requests accounts for some of the confusion felt by school authorities. But the more important explanation is that the parent who seeks bureaucratic permission for home schooling is asking an educational expert to empower a nonexpert. The lord of the institutional barony is being challenged on his own turf. A person whose work requires the manipulation of categories and the ignoring of individual characteristics is being asked to understand and acknowledge the needs and aspirations of one family. For the superintendent, it is a confusing and upsetting situation because it suggests that one of the school's major arguments for public acceptance—socializing children for survival in the society—is no longer convincing to parents.

In this situation of first impressions, it might be expected that the superintendent's initial task would be to learn as much as possible about the family's desires for the education of their child. In practice, this almost never happens. The superintendent may make inquiries of the school counsel or state education officials about his legal powers, but he will seek only minimal understanding of the family. The family is not taken seriously. Almost immediately it becomes objectified; it becomes a case that will not fit easily within existing categories, a wrinkle in the smooth operation of the bureaucracy, a nuisance.

Before seeking school approval, most families have been advised or have figured out that they cannot succeed by defiance and that they must appear reasonable and flexible at all times. Yet almost all parents sitting in a school superintendent's office feel insecure and more submissive than they would like to. There is as well a family defensiveness that is probably inevitable for people who recognize they are submitting their family for judgment by a public authority. The feelings that home-schooling advocates bring to their first encounter with school bureaucracy are probably similar to the feelings of other parents seeking to articulate the needs of their children in public schools.

In a study of the relationship between families and schools, *Worlds Apart*, Sara Lawrence Lightfoot observed and explored the thinking of parents who do not feel entitled to make demands of schools:

> The enduring historical experience of exclusion and oppression has made it difficult for the oppressed (be they

106

women, minorities, or the poor) to identify their *own* needs, desires, and goals. In order to survive, they have been forced into a preoccupation with sustaining the well being and scrutinizing the subtle behaviors and demands of the more powerful. The risks of identifying and asserting their own needs are great, and they fear that the enduring pain of long years of silence might explode into uncontrollable rage if they let it be exposed and released.

The parents have no better understanding of how the school bureaucracy works or how its personnel think than the superintendent has of the family's values, aspirations, or views of education. From the beginning, the situation is ripe for misunderstanding and conflict. On the issue of balance of power between family and school, disagreement is generated quickly. On the issue of the differing values, beliefs and world views reflected in education, there will be few questions and little understanding. It is as if this level—the most basic level of the problem—is so personal and so laced with issues of conscience and assumptions about the meaning of life, that it cannot be affected by rational evidence or resolved by any basically political process.

Objectively, and in terms of their own self-interest, superintendents have every reason to be supportive of the parents and to grant the required approval without fanfare or controversy. One family out of the thousands or even millions in a school system does not pose a threat to existing public-school practices. Not many families are likely to suddenly develop the desire to educate their children at home as a result of a favorable ruling for those who have already asked. Economically, the loss the local school system suffers is small, especially when compared to the economic sacrifice a family must make to provide home education. Finally, those families that have the financial and emotional resources to press legal cases against a disapproving school administrator generally win the right to home education. The cost to the superintendent of losing this battle in terms of legal fees, time and energy diverted from other matters, and adverse publicity hardly seems worth a victory, much less a precedent-setting loss.

Yet school superintendents and other school authorities charged with the task of evaluating home-education requests almost always find themselves involved in pitched conflict with a single family seeking to educate their children at home. The reasons behind the school authorities' combative actions and impractical reactions form a surprisingly prevalent pattern. It is a pattern of thought and behavior that is revealing of the cultural problems repeatedly being played out beneath the surface of home-education struggles.

When a family seeks approval of a home-education plan from a public authority, it is implicitly challenging the professionalization of education. Although most home-education families approach their local school superintendent with an awareness that the superintendent is a political animal, they know too that there are educational and certification requirements for the job, just as there are for the position of teacher. These "professional" attributes form the first barrier to good-faith discussions between family and school.

In order for education to be regarded as a profession, it has developed an image of expertise expressed in a specialized jargon, measured by "scientific" evaluation, taught in graduate schools by people with advanced degrees and federal grants, and made officially true and legally binding by a system of state certification. But educational research is rife with contradictions and uncertainties. Whether expertise is at all real or useful is a question seldom asked by professional educators, except when confronted with home-schooling parents.

Of course, the fragility of expertise in most professions is out of proportion to the demands for certainty and for solutions that the lay public makes of these professions. One parent, who had been through nearly three years of struggle with school professionals, first over curriculum and organization in the public school and then over a home-education plan for his son, put it this way: "No person but one within a profession knows the shallowness of that profession." In education, the fragility of expertise is greater than in most professions and so is the profession's awareness of this fragility. As a result, educators respond to general social pressure for expertise by turning every human interaction into a matter of technique and every area of work into an arcane and inaccessible specialization.

The professionalizing process rests upon the willingness—even the eagerness—of members of the general public to forfeit their self-confidence and their democratic control of some area of life. Many educators seem to regard their occupational survival as dependent upon their insistence that they, and only they, can adequately define, create, and judge quality education. Like lawyers, whose indispensability to society depends upon the continuous mystification of conflict, educators produce a system of language, power, arcane knowledge, and public insecurity about learning in order to be considered professional.

At meetings with school officials, many families soon discover that the doubts educators have about the genuineness of their profession are stirred up by those who propose home education. Ambivalence is not a useful characteristic for those who wield public power; yet the home-education family often evokes an educator's ambivalent feelings about his or her putative profession. This ambivalence is then suppressed by the educator's even more single-minded commitment to questioning the family's right and ability to educate a child at home.

These educators are not personally predisposed to denigrating other people or families or to expanding their own egos by playing on the fears of those who seek approval for home schooling. They are caught up in expectations—some of which are reinforced by the parents who trust their children to the schools thirty hours a week—that require school officials to appear to have the answers in order to relieve parents of the task of thinking about their children's education. The justifying of public expenditure for school bureaucracy becomes synonymous with displacing parents from their natural role as teachers. The inflation of professionalism becomes a natural means of assuring the majority of parents that their enormous emotional investment in schooling is yielding a tangible return.

Home-education families are fearful of judgment about their abilities as parents, just as educators are fearful of acknowledging their profession's tenuous hold on reality. These countervailing fears of judgment exaggerate the antagonism between the family and the superintendent and make genuine communication less and less likely. While the problem of evaluating a proposed home curriculum is seen as a muted threat of exposure for the paper-thin profession of education, the family's request is read as a revolt against the professionalization of life in general and of child rearing and the transmission of culture in particular. In response to these perceived challenges, the school authorities regard the families as socially disoriented aberrations. One mother summed up her year-long struggle over home education as an issue of "control of your own life." The school, she said, "is a machine that runs on acquiescence."

Just as the request for approval of home schooling expands into an issue of the educator's profession and professionalism, the attempt to fashion a study plan suited to one child expands into an attack on the suitability of the public school for all children. Although they usually try to avoid it, most parents find themselves drawn into a debate over the general quality of the public school. The preference of one family for educating its child at home is often heard by a school board or superintendent as a criticism of the local school system because these authorities are so accustomed to thinking about children in categories rather than as individuals. The system does not encourage—and cannot afford—addressing each child as unique. There are special programs, ability groups, levels, and tracks. But individual children or families do not exist. If the school is inappropriate for this child, then, *ipso facto,* it is not serving any of the children in the same category.

Often, parents who are trying to avoid criticizing the school system are asked if tests have been made to determine whether their child fits within one of the special-education or gifted-child categories. The response of the family is usually to resist the testing and labeling of the child; but most home-schooling families sense that it is unrealistic to ask that this categorical form of thought be abandoned and the idea that education is personal and individual be pursued. Time after time, the discussion between family and school official begins drifting into a debate over whether the child fits within one of the categories that form the basis of government schooling.

The result of the bureaucratic tendency to think about groups and ignore individuals is that whenever home instruction is suggested, the superintendent feels the need to defend the schools, while parents respond with attacks on schooling. To the school official, the modest achievements of children in school become the soaring accomplishments of a century of democratically run schools, publicly funded and publicly controlled. To the parents, the child's coerced conformity to a school's petty rules of behavior becomes a tragic history of the mutilation of childhood and a cause of the simultaneous deaths of learning and liberty. In the literature of education, there are enough books, studies, and expert opinions to show that both sides of this dispute are correct. The question of the adequacy of public schooling joins the threat to professionalism as a central theme underlying the growing conflict between family and school over one child's education at home.

These issues rarely are consciously recognized by the participants as influencing their positions. The typical home-schooling request leads to several meetings with school authorities during which the discussion of the proposed home-education plan comes to center on the vague notion of "equivalence" between the home curriculum and that supplied by the local public schools. The discussion of equivalence often serves to reinforce the existing tendencies to think about education in broad categorical terms; to regard the family request as an attack upon public schools in general; and to acquiesce in the professional judgment of the quality of schooling.

If the need to find equivalency exaggerates some problematic general attitudes about education, it also provides virtually no guidance about the balance of power between school and family. At opposite ends of the spectrum of possible interpretations of the meaning of equivalence, two things are clear: equivalence cannot mean "identity" or the constitutional right to an alternative to public schooling would become meaningless; and the family may not completely escape public education requirements or the term "equivalent education" would lose all force. In the vast gray area between these two extremes, the discretion of the school authorities has proved to be almost limitless.

Parents are typically unable to discover what standards the superintendent will apply in judging equivalence. The discussion about the issue therefore begins with the family at a psychological disadvantage. They are being judged on the basis of unknown standards. Worse still, the judgments that are eventually rendered are often devoid of the kind of information that might allow the family either to effectively dispute the judgment (with testimonials from its own educational experts) or change the proposed program to make it acceptable. Many parents regard these broad statements about the inadequacy of their proposed teaching methods, subjects of study, goals, and teaching abilities as a backdoor method for the superintendent to impose upon the family the idiosyncratic education philosophy or the moral and political values of the school system. Given the confusion in education literature about what methods produce what results and given the substantial differences in attitudes and beliefs of family and superintendent, the parents' suspicion can hardly be considered paranoid.

In the Amherst superintendent's memorandum denying the Perchemlideses approval for home education, three specific grounds were given: First, that the parents, both of whom are college educated, did not show information about "training or background appropriate to the task" proposed; second, that there was no "curricular sequence" in the thirty-page home-study plan; and third, that the plan provided "no opportunity to develop group skills with children of his age."

In an equally uninformative denial of home education in another state, the local superintendent informed the school board that the proposed home-education plan "would in no way be comparable to the total program of our public school," considering the school's "special teachers in music, art, physical education . . ." and the "countless items of media . . . and other equipment available in a formal school setting."

Both of these rejections were later overturned by higher authorities but without adding any substantial clarity to the permissible content of the Trojan horse, "equivalence."

Even the superintendent may be uncomfortable with the official view of equivalence he has generated in response to a home-education request. Local school officials are under growing restrictions from state and federal authorities who may prescribe courses to be taught; hours and days of required attendance; regulations for the hiring, transfer, or firing of teachers; tests to be given and special programs to be established. Further, declining birth rates and inflation put school authorities under extreme pressure to extend their near monopoly over schooling as a means of compensating for projected loss of clients and resources. A siege mentality is generated. One can almost read the internal monologue between the lines of home-education rejections: "If I have to struggle with these bureaucratic restrictions, there is no justification for allowing individual families to escape them." The availability of a wide area of discretion for the superintendent in approval of home education provides an opportunity for an overrestricted superintendent to become the regulator rather than the regulated. The appearance of a family requesting approval of home instruction has often become a lightning rod for many of the frustrations endured by the employees of highly bureaucratized public schools. The superintendent is probably doing the best that can be done with a bad situation as he or she attempts to keep the public schools running smoothly. Being confronted with people who feel they can do better by avoiding the very bureaucracy that defines the superintendent's work rubs many school authorities the wrong way.

The meeting with the school authorities is traumatic for the family because they have a sense that under the civility and vagueness of the process there are deep institutional and professional forces that will prevent a direct discussion of the issue they care most about—home schooling for the child. At the core of this problem is an almost insoluble dilemma—the clash of individuality with institutional patterns of thought and activity. The home-schooling family's symbolic significance—a significance conferred on it by society—creates this dilemma. The family has its own beliefs about the world, its own ideas of success, failure, survival, and conscience, and, in some cases, its own philosophy of education and life. The family does not wish to be incorporated into a school, regulated by a political majority, or manipulated by a bureaucracy. In fact, in most instances with which I am familiar, the family, no matter how religious, does not wish to identify with the formal theology of an organized church in its struggle for home education. Yet in response to these assertions of individualism, the school authority can muster only bureaucratized perceptions and regulated responses.

The clash of individualism and schooling is fundamental. In classroom and curriculum the school preaches respect for the individual. In the legislature, the media, and much scholarship the school system justifies itself historically as a teacher of the democratic value of individual dignity. The point is well made by Diane Ravitch in her book, *The Revisionists Revised*: "The democratic-liberal tradition argues for an education that respects the worth and dignity of each individual, that prizes freedom of inquiry and expression, and that enables each person to think and participate and choose independently." Yet the reality of managing and

114

teaching in public school makes the recognition of individualism impossible and threatening. The structure of schooling transforms the ideology of schooling into hypocrisy. It is no wonder school authorities react defensively and irrationally to requests for home instruction.

The family that seeks permission to educate its children at home has unearthed a longstanding contradiction in American society. A history of individual autonomy and independent action has been all but buried by the inevitable institutionalization of life functions; yet individualism remains a central part of American consciousness. The more the expectation of individual effectiveness and the ideology of individual dignity are touted, the less they are observed in social structure. The more an individual insists upon recognition, the more tense and uncomfortable institutional managers become about their inability to respond to that individual. The home-schooling family makes us conscious of this painful contradiction between ideology and practice.

Education is expected to harmonize and integrate ideals with reality, to oversee the development of beliefs and their extension into life. That is the meaning of socialization in schooling and its central purpose in the public mind and judicial opinions. In schooling, therefore, the contradiction between individualistic beliefs and institutional activity is hardened; and those whose actions expose this contradiction to public examination are met by irrational and oppressive reactions from school authorities. What the late twentieth century home-schooling family is discovering is that not only is there no room for its peculiar values and beliefs but that the dilemma of individualism in an institutional society is so tension ridden that it paralyzes social action and fragments cultural beliefs.

In spite of this tension, it is in superficial civility that the opposing parties find one of their few agreements. Even later, when the harshness of the school authorities' actions becomes evident in the filing of criminal charges or welfare department custody orders, most parents acknowledge that all parties are sincere and that no individual is to blame for

115

the consequences of increasingly polarized positions. In order to preserve a nice-guy posture, school authorities often deny their personal responsibility by invoking the requirements of law. The reliance on "law" evokes obedience where the professional authority of the superintendent or the school board is not persuasive. The use of law reflects the degree to which the schools already feel beleaguered by constant value conflict and by legal restrictions that have become substitutes for a community of values.

Legal restrictions on home education are endlessly flexible. Hiding behind the law serves two related functions: It escalates the family's fear of authority as a means of gaining their acquiescence; and it provides an outlet for the superintendent's own fear of authority by allowing an escape from personal responsibility. In one midwestern city, a superintendent about to embark on the second criminal prosecution of a home-schooling family asked the county attorney to tell him that prosecution was required by law. The county attorney refused, pointing out that it was the school board's duty to decide what course of action to take and the attorney's duty to effectuate it once it was decided. The superintendent was flabbergasted.

School superintendents who behave in this way do not have as their purpose preventing home schooling or arresting parents or legitimizing the kidnapping of children. Their evil is more mundane. They are unable to take responsibility for the consequences of their decisions. These consequences for the individual family that does not fit neatly into prearranged bureaucratic school categories include being subjected to deep emotional stress, being denied educational aspirations, and, ultimately, being deprived of family liberty and belief.

Yet the bureaucrats claim to be doing only what the law requires or what is "in the best interest of the child." There is no real connection between the denial of a home-education request and its effect on the family making the request. This submersion of person in role makes a mockery of ethics and elevates amorality to the status of virtue. Just

116

when parents seek to take responsibility for transmitting family culture and providing education for their children, the bureaucrat denies them. In the process he refuses to take responsibility for his own actions. This is what Jonathan Kozol calls "ethical numbness," the constantly recurring theme that the public has a stake in the repression of awakening consciences.

Once discussions have taken place and home study plans have been written, submitted, and evaluated, the superintendent or school board makes a decision about equivalence and general compliance with the requirements of compulsory education. Having been denied its request, the family, sharpened in its desire for home education and stiffened in its resistance to institutional schooling, must prepare for the formal legal action the schools will eventually take. The mutated family has failed to find a niche in the ecology of bureaucracy. It must now try—without this niche—to survive in the more confusing realm of the law.

II
Endangered Species:

THE PUBLIC REACTION
TO HOME EDUCATION

In spite of the strains imposed by prolonged uncertainty
and conflict with school authorities, most dissenting families
continue to value their independence and are nourished by a
growing sense of moral and intellectual correctness. In continuing to pursue the right of home education, the dissenting family becomes a catalyst for the expression of public
attitudes toward government schooling. In effect, it becomes
possible to reconstruct the ideology of American schooling
through the reactions of laymen and professionals to local
struggles for home education. A small amount of support
for, and opposition to, dissenting families comes to the surface of the home-education conflict. But the general public
reaction must be deciphered from private discussions with
members of the community.

On the positive side, dissenting families report receiving
supportive and sympathetic reactions including letters,
small contributions for legal fees, unsolicited advice, and
requests for help from other families. With the help of John
Holt's newsletter, *Growing without Schooling,* loose networks
of mutual aid and information sharing have cropped up in

various states and, on an *ad hoc* basis, across state lines. Some groups have offered expertise in curriculum planning or legal issues. Most of this technical help comes from outside the immediate community. The press and the electronic media contribute to the development of a second kind of support by presenting the local conflict as a David and Goliath battle, which in some ways it is, or as a campaign by peculiar dissenters to avoid the majority's pattern of life, which in some ways is also true. Under these circumstances some people come to identify with the family as underdogs standing up for themselves against the oppressive pressures of institutions and inaccessible authority. The dissenting family acts out common frustrations and desires, allowing the more timid to participate vicariously or just observe the struggle between individualism and the institutionalization of daily life.

Politicians are even more cautious about their reactions, and little can be learned from them about prevailing attitudes toward schooling. One education commissioner observed that home-education conflicts were so much a part of the general problem of relations between family and state that his office could devise no regulations or guidelines to help resolve the home-schooling conflict until the general political trend became clear. The caution of such politicians reflects the fact that the question of how public education ought to be structured and what attitude government should express toward family autonomy are just below the surface of public debate.

Open antipathy toward home-schooling families is detectable but on a scale as small as open support. The families report no overt acts of antagonism from private citizens, but letters to the editors of local papers and conversations with some community leaders indicate that some people feel that home schoolers have deeply insulted the communities in which they live. For some people, the idea that the public school is "not good enough" for a dissenting family means that there must be something crazy or irresponsible about the home-schooling family. By going public with their desire for approval of home education, these families have exposed themselves to some hypercritical judgments about the quality of their lives. They become fair game, as do many public figures, for the projective moralism and intolerance of those who believe that there is "one right way" to organize families, raise children, and operate schools.

The feeling that home education insults the community also arises from a sincerely held belief that publicly run schooling, however imperfect, is a major achievement of community cooperation and a significant expression of the process of community building. From this point of view, those who opt out of the school system do more than just reject the values that currently appear to hold sway among the general public; they refuse to acknowledge any obligation to participate in public value formation on its most local and accessible level. Worse than simply being dissenters or antiboosters, these individualistic families do not accept the argument that society may use child rearing as a process for creating and recreating group cohesion. The idea that the public can validly involve itself in nonreligious indoctrination and belief formation through schooling is at the heart of civic pride in public schools.

Those who support using public schools to foster community cohesion are aware that the agreement about values and beliefs that is supposed to underlie the structure, practice, and curriculum of public schools (if it is an agreement and not an imposition by a special-interest group) is tenuous. They fear that too many competing beliefs expressed too openly will shatter the fragile consensus that allows government-run schools to be regarded as public institutions. Requests for home schooling thus heighten public confusion about which beliefs are really valid expressions of community sentiment. By requiring public choices among diverse private consciences, majoritarian control of public schools creates the appearance of a unity that is refuted by the presence of home schoolers.

The majority of people in those communities experiencing conflict over home schooling refrain from publicly ex-

120

pressing either sympathy or antipathy for the dissenting family. But the silence of the majority does not indicate disinterest, at least if the level of television, radio, and press coverage and the private comments of local people can be taken as indications. It has proved impossible to gain direct access to the thoughts of those who watch home-schooling conflicts with detached concern, though these people are undoubtedly the backbone of support for public schools and for the superintendents who prosecute dissenting families in the public's name. But a series of discussions with public-school authorities, educators, education writers, civil libertarians, and others who are accustomed to articulating and influencing the views of the silent majority does yield some strikingly common themes. By putting all these comments together, one can discern an outline of some elements of the ideology of public education as put in relief by home-schooling conflicts. Much of this ideology is shared by liberals and conservatives alike. Home-schooling controversies in effect bring out the ideological defense of government schooling:

1. The problem of conflict between families and schools is one of balancing the interests of the two. Parents do have important rights and responsibilities, but society has the predominant responsibility for family morals and beliefs. It is more appropriate for any family to concern itself with the general education of children in society than with the particular education of its own children. To do otherwise is selfish.

2. One of the obligations of the public that can legitimately be carried out through school policy is the protection of children from "bad" parenting. There are a lot of crazy parents out there who will ruin their children and block their development as healthy individuals if the schools do not provide a counterbalance to their influence. Conflict between parental and school influence on children aids the development of a child's independence and freedom of thought.

3. Many families are conflict ridden themselves and will impose their tensions on their children if parental influence is undiluted by schooling, whether public or private. As children become more mature, they will have preferences and judgments different from those of their parents. Home schooling does not respect the right of children to differ from parents and imposes an even more rigid orthodoxy upon a dissenting child than any school system could.

4. School is an essential force for social cohesion. Any right of parents to home education outside of approved public morality creates a clear danger of social fragmentation. Religious fanaticism, racism, anarchism, and other evils would result if the process of political compromise over school issues were abandoned. Even a bureaucratized public order is preferable to chaos or anarchy. The social order implied by the values of some dissenting families is intolerable to the majority, which can rightfully protect itself against cultural subversion.

5. The socialization of children in groups is essential. Only through peer-group schooling can children learn to get along in a highly interdependent society.

6. The mixing of children from different backgrounds and from families with differing beliefs and values is vital to peace in a pluralistic socity. Without the mixing of children in schools, adults would not respect each other's differences.

7. The adequate functioning of the American democratic system requires that every child be taught the values of liberty as well as the skills of literacy. Coercion in the name of liberty is valid. Compulsory socialization does not interfere with academic learning.

8. Children who are educated at home may become hermits deprived of the skills needed for economic survival and political participation. These children may become a social burden in a complex society and may be deprived of economic opportunity. The society can justifiably protect itself against these costs through its school system.

9. Teachers have a genuine, certifiable expertise that

many parents lack. The protection of children from inadequate teaching is a compelling public concern.

What all of these elements of the liberal ideology of schooling amount to is an attempt to define what David Tyack has called (in his book by the same name) "the one best system." These educators share a general distrust of parents and a view that it is possible, desirable, and even essential to prescribe a system of values that is best for everyone. The assumption is that each family must adhere to the minimum in child rearing in order to qualify for the right to dissent in other areas. The culture, the political system, and the state have the right to preserve themselves through government schooling. Those families that insist that home education is a part of the fundamental right of citizens to dissent in belief and belief formation are in the minority and, in the environment of school ideology, constitute an endangered species.

12

Unnatural Selection:

THE COURT HEARING

Most dissenting families whose commitment to home schooling is strong enough to sustain them in a struggle with a powerful school bureaucracy are undaunted by that bureaucracy's denial of their request for official approval. Typically, the child has been taken out of school before the home-education request was made and has remained at home during its p/endency, a period of as much as a year in some cases. During the struggle the parents have had to explain and defend their views on education so many times to school authorities, the press, friends, and themselves that an increased clarity of belief appears and a firmer sense that home schooling is right for their children takes hold in the family. Even those families that began home schooling on an impulse or with only a vague, antistate ideology have by now developed an articulate criticism of institutional schooling.

Not only has the behavior of the school authorities thus far failed to convince the family to return the child to school, it has fulfilled some of the family's worst fears about government. Through widespread albeit unintentional insensitivity to their individual values and needs, the school has convinced the family that individual education and institutional schooling do not mix. By overwhelming the family's vision of survival with self-serving professionalism and a bureaucratic defense of public orthodoxy, the superintendent has confirmed the parents' fear that the people exist for the government and not the government for the people.

The dissenting family waits tensely, trying to go on with its home education while the school authorities examine the tools of compulsion available to them. Although in some states the finality of a superintendent's home-education ruling may be delayed by an appeal to a state board of education, ultimately, the chief school officer will choose a mechanism to enforce his or her decision. That mechanism may be criminal prosecution for violation of the compulsory education statute, a family court order to return the child to an approved school, or a petition filed formally by the welfare department to remove custody of the child from the parents for "neglect."

Since it is likely to be common knowledge that parents have served prison terms or lost custody of their children while spending large sums on legal defense, these possibilities display the sharp edge of intimidation. Still, prior to formal legal action, civility and a veneer of respect for the family's sincerity are usually maintained. If harsh and divisive measures are being considered by the superintendent, it is suggested that it is not personal animosity that motivates him but an avowed duty to enforce the law.

In spite of the apparent good faith, the polarization of positions begins to increase, compromise becomes less and less likely, and the conflict takes on a life of its own. Personal and institutional views of cultural survival, of adequate education, of what is best for the child all begin to fade. The preparation for a legal battle makes the issue more abstract. It makes power the issue between the parties. A desire for vindication is often added to the emotions with which everyone must deal. The school bureaucracy moves slowly, but in many cases it moves inevitably toward bringing the family into a court where, in effect, a judge will be asked to select whose values are fit to survive. Under this kind of stress, and considering their lack of financial resources, it is remarkable how few families seek to escape the legalization of conflict.

The form in which the conflict appears in court varies from the common criminal prosecutions and child custody contests to civil actions sometimes brought by the family to terminate government harassment and secure the desired right of home education. Whichever path is taken the problem usually is reduced to a single, two-part question: How much power does an individual family have over the education of its own children?; and what, if any, restrictions will the law impose on the discretion of school authorities to regulate home schooling? Nearly sixty years ago in a private-school case, the Supreme Court affirmed the constitutional right of families to choose an alternative to public schooling and declared that "the child is not the mere creature of the state." That began, rather than ended, the problem of allocating power over value socialization in schooling, for the court has also affirmed the authority of the government to make some regulation of nonpublic schooling. The parties to home-education litigation are confronted with the need to clarify constitutional ambiguities over fifty years old and to settle with public law what they have been unable to agree upon in private discussion.

A surprising number of families involved in this type of court action choose to represent themselves, at least initially. "The politicians are almost always lawyers, and look what a mess they have made of things," one father commented. But the motivation to conduct their own defense does not seem to be a concern that an attorney will not adequately represent the family's position. It is, rather, consistent with their individualism for a family to represent itself in court. There is a feeling that the Constitution and individual rights mean more than lawyers make it mean, just as education means more than school superintendents make it mean. The threads that run through home-schooling and self-representation decisions are the desire for independence and self-sufficiency and a distrust of institutions.

The spotty history of home-education litigation over the past five years includes some cases that have been decided against dissenting families and some that have ended in victory for the families. But none provides a significant change in the substance or clarity of the law affecting home education. Typically, a parent will be acquitted of a truancy charge and wind up continuing home schooling while the next round of charges is prepared. Only a few cases rise above the magistrate or probate court levels to be heard in state appeals courts. These require even greater financial expenditures from the family and school authorities, more sophisticated legal representation, the use of "expert" testimony, and an attempt to set a precedent for other home-schooling cases. Those families that are able to go this far down the predictable path of the home-schooling conflict are transforming their private dissent into a question of importance to the entire public.

Most courts do not like to have to deal with education cases, especially home-education cases. The issue is relatively new. Most of the judges who see these cases believe they know almost nothing about education, though they generally have children of their own and may even have served on local school boards. The professionalism claimed by school superintendents is not without its effect on these judges who can be counted on to resist the "legalization" of social institutions claiming specialized knowledge. The problem of decision-making fairness—of whether due process was afforded the dissenting family—may be the only area in which judicial authority is comfortably exercised on school issues. Beyond this, most courts are predisposed by the ideology of law to avoid choosing among education values and to accept the expertise of school authorities as determinative. Courts in general will more readily legitimize an institution's rules than question their wisdom. A court's decision about which home-education plans will survive is therefore reduced to the question of school-board power, which does not require knowledge of education or concern for family liberties other than due process.

During the typical legal proceeding each side will seek to convince the court that it should be granted the balance of power over the child's education. Each will provide a rationalization for the court to adopt if it decides in its favor. The school's position evolves from a grant of power by the state requiring that public schools be provided and that every child within a certain age range be educated in a satisfactory manner. The grant of power includes an unspecified amount of control over alternatives to the public schools. Whatever specific criteria may be found in the statutes, the school will argue that the proper reading of the statute grants it discretion to interpret and enforce standards for all schooling, that the family's plan does not meet these standards, and, sometimes, that no justifications need be given at all by school superintendents for their negative decisions. The bureaucracy assumes it has limitless legal powers and its lawyers defend that assumption.

The family's position is to claim that the state or federal government guarantees each family the fundamental right to control the education of its children, just as it guarantees religious freedom or freedom of expression. The power of the state to establish minimum regulations is generally acknowledged by the dissenting family, but they insist that the school has overstepped this minimum and is infringing on the family's privacy by overregulating its freedom of belief. Minimum standards must be just that, it is argued, and they may be created only for the most compelling of reasons.

In reply, the schools argue that the family has a clear right to attend a private school but that the proposed home-education plan does not meet the "equivalency" standard the school board must legally apply. The family will then claim that "equivalence to public instruction" is merely a subterfuge for arbitrarily imposing the majority's or the superintendent's education philosophy and for regulating out of existence the family's constitutional right to an alternative to public school. Evidence will be introduced by the

128

family to show that their home curriculum is within professional, accepted standards of quality and that the superintendent must therefore have gone beyond the bounds of equivalence in refusing approval.

Testing and evaluation often become a sticking point in this general argument about the relative power of the dissenting family and the school authority. In some instances the family will offer the results of standardized tests to show that not only is their home education program equivalent, but its measurable results are better than those achieved within the public system.

Here the school authorities will shift from output to input as a standard of judgment and argue that there are other factors, such as available materials or group experiences, important to judging educational equivalence. Other families totally reject the idea that standardized tests can measure anything significant about an educational experience. Many feel that testing is biased ethnically, that it distorts the learning process, is intimidating to the child, and, inevitably, becomes a means of imposing required content through required testing. As one parent put it during his struggle to have an alternative to testing accepted as evaluation, "Testing is like pulling up a plant by its roots to see if it is still growing." When testing is rejected by a dissenting family, it seems to become all the more important to the school authorities who typically reject test scores as a form of accountability for themselves and their teachers.

The self-serving interests of all parties in testing is only a small part of an issue that plagues schools, families, and education policy makers everywhere. At bottom it is a problem of the goals of education. Even when agreement can be reached on a reliable and fair means of measuring the attainment of a particular goal, the conflict persists over what the proper goals are, who should be accountable for them, and, in some cases, whether education might not simply be the kind of activity, like life in general, that ought to have no prescribed goals. The technological problem of measuring learning and the philosophical problem of attaching goals to

129

education are especially acute where individual family dissent confronts categorized school-system policy. Emotions run high, for example, over the proper meaning of a legal precedent that the goal of the compulsory attendance statute in Massachusetts is "that all children shall be educated, but not that they shall be educated in any particular way." The testing issue, like the equivalence issue, is ultimately a debate about value inculcation and belief formation in children.

The legal issues of public-school equivalency, evaluation, and due process form the surface of the court contest. The social symbols that lie just below this surface are more powerful and are rarely dealt with by the law. School superintendents become the symbolic defenders of their profession, the institution of public schooling, the primacy of institutions over individuals, the majoritarian prerogative in democratic society, and the obedience to authority in general.

The dissenting family carries as its symbolic baggage the defense of a child's intellectual and ethical future, a family's right to believe whatever it pleases about the world, individual independence, family solidarity, a radical critique of compulsory schooling, and an antistate political philosophy.

These interests, and the feelings that go along with them, are brought into court wrapped in the garb of the few legal precedents that will actually be considered. It is a tight fit. Most of the issues the conflict raises will not be resolved or even addressed. All that can be done is to indicate whether, in this case, school authority has exceeded its power. The fear of dealing with the transmission of culture, of questioning the expertise of educators, and of upsetting the fragile public consensus on school values makes superficial issues the only manageable issues. The basic allocation of individual liberty and institutional power, like the detailed problems of this family and this school system and the cultural struggle they symbolize, are left untouched.

The process is an unnatural selection of the survivors because so much that matters to other families, to school authorities, and to the public will be untouched by the court.

130

Even if the family wins, a great deal of discretion is typically left in the hands of the school authorities to continue using approval standards as a means of preventing families from pursuing their own vision of survival through home education. In *Perchemlides* v. *Frizzle* the superior court ruled that the dissenting family had a right to choose home education, unfettered by school board judgments about family motivations or the lack of group experiences for the child. But in sending the issue back for reconsideration to the school department of Amherst, the court stated that such a reconsideration could take into account the competency of parents as teachers; the manner in which required subjects are taught and whether they "impart comparable knowledge as given in the local schools"; and "the adequacy of texts, materials, methods, and programs being used." Evaluation prescribed by the superintendent and based on the family's goals was permitted. It was a victory for the Perchemlides family but not for home schooling in general.

Up to this point no major court has struck a clear and comprehensible balance between the power of the family and the power of the school to control the education of the child. When such an occasion does finally arrive, the court will not succeed in resolving the conflict over home education unless it abandons attention to superficial issues and takes up the question of whether the right to preserve family values and privacy is so fundamental, and the right to an alternative to public school so basic to freedom of belief, that the state must have a compelling justification for any regulation it makes of home education.

Even with a willingness to address the central issues forthrightly, a court may have difficulty perceiving the clash of values and beliefs that powers the contest it is attempting to resolve. When, as so often happens, a dissenting family is able to describe its values more readily in terms of what it rejects in the public sphere than in terms of what it believes privately, the conflict will appear as lopsided. Moreover, because it is easier to describe values as attributes of a large, functioning group than of a single family, the home-

131

education family seeking the freedom to develop its values and share them voluntarily with others will present the most difficult case for the courts.

Until a case exploring the constitutional magnitude and cultural significance of home schooling is argued and decided, home-schooling conflicts will continue, and issues of personal conscience and institutional power will produce a level of strife that will threaten institutional stability and undermine family life.

The courts have provided little help not only because the adversary process is so brittle and the depth of the issues evoked by home education so little understood but because the alternative solutions available to the court are so limited. One school-board member who voted against a home-education plan stated his opposition to having the matter resolved in court as follows: "Judges do not have the flexibility needed for a creative solution. Just like the rest of us, their education did not teach them to think of alternatives." It may be that, as this comment implies, a nonadversarial form such as mediation would be more likely to successfully resolve individual home education disputes than would formal court proceedings. But mediation might be incapable of resolving the competing beliefs, attitudes, and world views at the core of the problem of whether the state should have substantial control over family-education decisions.

Families whose lives have begun to follow the predictable path of the struggle for home schooling have paid a heavy personal price to expose an essentially public issue. In many instances family fabric has tightened in response to the struggle, but the toll in emotional and financial resources has been large. The strain of having one's children at risk and one's daily life preoccupied is more than most people can tolerate. The rejection of the easy support of institutionalized life, in order to attain independence and perhaps isolation, is not a trade-off attractive to many families struggling to survive. For most people the thought of confronting the power of the state produces more anxieties than insights.

In spite of these intimidating costs, most families who have stuck with the struggle through appellate court proceedings feel that, on balance, they have gained by their experiences. They have learned an enormous amount about schooling, about themselves, and about political reality. The struggle for family survival has strengthened them emotionally. One father noticed that after a year of fighting for his own constitutional right he had developed a much clearer sense of the meaning of individual liberty and a stronger commitment to his beliefs. So clear did his sense become that he began to notice he was violating other people's rights in the ordinary practice of his work as a police officer. When he extended his new-found ideology to his work and refused to take actions he believed were in violation of a citizen's constitutional rights, he found himself in trouble with his superiors and co-workers. For families like this the struggle over schooling does not end; it extends itself as a form of dissent into other areas of institutional life. The strength and independence of families struggling against public orthodoxy is a notable contrast to the prevailing passivity of their neighbors.

The final irony of the home-education struggle lies in the individualism these families assert so vehemently and school authorities find so painful. A few families, having rejected institutionally formed and maintained values in order to practice and pass on their own beliefs, are now searching for a wider community of shared values.

There is little temptation to return to the school community, which they regard as artificial and bureaucratically imposed. There is some temptation to look back to one's ethnic or religious roots, but these are regarded as having been transcended or as having lost much of their legitimacy. But there is an effort to conduct schooling within some community and thereby ease the isolation of extreme individualism and extended struggle with the state.

There is also a perception that knowledge is created and preserved by collective life as much as it is produced by individual thought. This tentative and experimental recognition that education must take place within a community of shared values in order to gain its full impact and use contrasts sharply with the individualism that originally motivated the home-schooling decision. At the very least, the communitarian thinking of educational individualists suggests that social cohesion, no matter how essential to life and education, cannot be created by coercive state intervention and that bureaucratic order cannot substitute for a lack of community.

III
SUBCULTURE
AND THE STATE

The state is the alienated form of society . . .

—Stanley Diamond

Those who are not attracted by the isolation of home education and who cannot win the zero-sum game of public-school orthodoxy may seek out private schooling. As with home education, some extra financial or emotional resources are required, and it is rarely the impoverished, the victims of discrimination, or the overworked who can afford private schools. Part Three presents the struggle of one group of people that has sought to preserve an unorthodox subculture through control of socialization in their own schools. Chapter 13 sketches the struggles of two groups—the Amish of Wisconsin and a multiracial countercultural group in Santa Fe, New Mexico—in order to describe the general attitude of government officials toward private education in the last decade. Chapters 14, 15, and 16 detail the conflict between Christian fundamentalists and the school authorities of Kentucky over the survival of a subculture whose beliefs do not meet with state approval. In Chapter 17 it is suggested that in spite of its magnitude, the fundamentalist victory does not bode well for other subcultures because of the judiciary's current conception of freedom of belief.

13

Conflict over Community

Men had better be without education than be educated by their rulers.

—Thomas Hodgskin, 1823

In September of 1968 Jonas Yoder and two other Amish residents of Wisconsin refused to send their children to high school, claiming that the informal education in the close-knit Amish community was all these children needed for a sane life now and salvation later. The New Glarus, Wisconsin, public-school administrator did not see life or education this way. As a result, Yoder and the others faced criminal charges and possible prison sentences. Their simple act of conscience, based on religious beliefs, was characterized not only as a violation of compulsory attendance laws but as a threat to public education and to the future of majority culture. Ultimately, the state Attorney General's office, the state Supreme Court, the U.S. Supreme Court and one of the nation's leading constitutional lawyers became involved in determining whether the Amish community's right to survival outweighed the interest of the state in de-

137

termining what constituted good education for all its citizens.

The nature of the Amish community as symbolized by Jonas Yoder and the nature of mainstream American culture as represented by the local and state school authorities in this case could not be more different. According to the attorney who argued the "plain people's" case before the U.S. Supreme Court, "The purpose of Amish education is not to get ahead in the world but to get to heaven." For three centuries the Amish have been dissenters from the culture of social and technological progress, seeking to live as much like early Christians as possible. As a simple religious community, they view formal schooling of adolescents as a worldly threat to their values; and, consistent with this belief, practice a separation from the modern world that helps preserve a coherent and self-sufficient community. The Amish use no modern conveniences and therefore contribute to none of the world's modern plagues. They cause no pollution, use no electricity, drive no cars, and watch no television. Neither war nor litigation is a part of their highly collectivized and tightly knit community. They are, in a way that touches the cultural memory of Americans, puritanical.

Their religious beliefs hold that a child is baptized as a teenager upon deciding to take the religious community as his or her own. This view is held by a community in which religious values pervade everyday life and in which the church is not a building, but a characteristic of everyday life. In this community of faith there is none of the paralyzing skepticism of mainstream American culture.

The progress of the Amish compulsory schooling case reveals that the Amish community is both attractive and threatening to the society at large, and for the same reasons. Amish life is peaceful, simple, clean, pious, and temperate. These characteristics are an attractive contrast to the anxieties and fears many outsiders feel about their constantly changing and ambiguous existence. The union of simple faith and practical success is enviable. Yet the claim of the Amish to be free of a material vision of the good life and to be exempt from the compulsory schooling that is supposed to perpetuate that life is also insulting. Those who believe they have no alternative to the rat race sense that the Amish road may be right but that it cannot be reached from the land of sophisticated and material wealth. The clash between the Amish community and public education is not simply about what type of education best prepares children for a meaningful life but about what constitutes a meaningful life.

In January of 1971 the New Mexico Department of Education disapproved the secondary education program of the Santa Fe Community School, an open classroom, multiracial, antiauthoritarian, and countercultural project of local families and teachers. By the summer of 1971 the state had increased its program of harassment, threatening to enforce the truancy laws against families whose children attended the school and publicly malign the reputation of the school. In February of 1972, after the failure of the school to negotiate a truce with the state authorities, the Santa Fe Community School filed suit in the New Mexico state court, claiming that the state Board of Education had no legal authority to regulate and control private schools at all and that their attempt to do so violated the freedom of belief and expression of the school community. The state responded by disapproving the school's elementary program as well. It took two years and, in the words of the school's director, "one thousand hours of legal preparation, ten attorneys, thirty-six specific complainants, fourteen defendants, six judges, two courts, . . . and the time-consuming review of two legislative committees, both houses of the state legislature, and the governor" before the issue was resolved, temporarily, in favor of the Santa Fe Community School.

The issue in New Mexico was culture versus counterculture. It was a struggle between a small group of people searching, tentatively, for a way of learning and living that reflected their desire for something better than business as usual and a state education bureaucracy that could not credit the validity of any approach to education or life that varied

139

from its rules and regulations. The actions of the bureaucracy faced the Community School squarely with the fact that public school does educate kids for certain aspects of life in America and that the families of the SFCS reject both that life and training for it. The SFCS had to fight in court to preserve its ability to formulate and pass on an antistate world view. Here is how the school's "message to posterity" was described in the book they wrote about their struggle, *Cheez! Uncle Sam*:

> You can be free here, yes; but the price is more than you can afford to pay, and the package you take home will be empty. You can learn to understand and come to believe in the value of democratic decision-making now, but decisions that control your lives will be made later in society without your consent, by a bureaucratic process that practices and supports authoritarian rule in the functions of all its public institutions . . . Your children yet unborn will one day be sentenced to twelve years of subtle indoctrination and control; they will be compelled to believe in blind obedience to authority, powerless and incapable of conscious response even to their own urgent needs . . . Unless we fight back against the prevalence and privilege of the public school monopoly . . . then there is no bequest, no reason for our existence, no hope for real freedom for children in this society.

The Santa Fe Community School could not describe its fledgling values in religious terms or lay claim to 300 years of practice or present itself as a throwback to the values of early American Puritanism. But this green bud of a community was clearly involved in a conflict between a vision of culture it practiced and taught and one embedded in the bureaucratic mind. The SFCS rejects authoritarianism, competition, exploitation of environment, classism, and fragmentation of learning. The depth and centrality of the values shared by the members of the Santa Fe Community School can be gauged by the sacrifices they made to preserve their tiny community of children and adults. The extent of the threat felt by the public school authorities can be measured by the time, expense, and trouble to which they went in an attempt to stamp out a group of impoverished families and teachers which never amounted to more than one hundred people all together.

As these brief sketches suggest, both families and public officials in charge of education regard schools as places in which culture is transmitted and, in the process, defined. Control of the school means control of one important and accessible means by which one generation passes its heritage to the next. In the view of some families who seek to avoid the battle over orthodoxy in government schools, nongovernment schooling can sometimes be used to establish or to maintain a community of belief and to transmit subculture. These voluntary associations constitute a form of group dissent from majority culture and politics. The question raised by the struggles of small communities of belief against state control is whether the seeds of subculture can survive the political environment of American schooling and the attitudes of the public toward education.

To gain a general understanding of the effect of majority control of schooling in America on subcultures, we must ask whether conflict over the regulation of nongovernment schools constitutes an attempt by the state, however unintentional, to prevent the formation of competing ideologies or to thwart the creation of communities of belief. This part of the book deals with how would-be communities learned the hard way that the structure of American schooling is no more hospitable to group dissent than it is to individual dissent and that the tendency of the state is to cannibalize subcultures through the use of law. The struggle between Christian schools in Kentucky and state educators reviewed here is a modern example of this tendency. Before detailing the story, however, some background on the regulation of nongovernment schools will be useful.

A dozen years ago the prevailing wisdom about government's relationship to private schools was that there was little need for any but the most minimal regulation. A review of the legal status of private-school regulation, which was part of a general study of *Public Controls for Nonpublic Schools* (Donald Erickson, Ed., 1969), disclosed that states varied widely in the types of requirements they imposed but that none had systematically addressed the area of regulation in the absence of specific incidents demonstrating the need for regulation. The percentage of students attending private schools was relatively stable, and the use of private schooling to challenge the prevailing values of the majority had only just begun to be noticed publicly. Those who did articulate concern about the relationship of state school authorities to subculture and counterculture focused mainly upon preventing private schools from securing a share of state education funds. There was some concern over hucksterism in proprietary schools but no more than the level of concern over conventional forms of commercial exploitation of consumers.

Before the sixties some people may have sought to use private schools to transmit dissenting values and thereby maintain the cohesiveness of one group or another. The general posture of state education authorities toward nongovernment schools has remained a laissez-faire one. Two Supreme Court cases in the twenties had provided some protection to private schools, but since that time few cases involving state regulation of these schools had reached the courts, except where aid to religious schools was concerned. Perhaps educators in the public sector were too concerned with their own burgeoning problems and enrollments to worry much over the problems of nonpublic schools. Perhaps an abundance of jobs for teachers in the public schools meant little concern for the conditions of the profession in nonpublic schools. There were few full-blown conflicts over what was being taught or learned in private schools.

Since the late sixties public control of private schooling has become more of an issue. Public-school enrollments began to decline while inflation ate into their budgets and reduced the number of teaching jobs. Proposals for tuition vouchers, tax credits, and other schemes for sharing tax revenues among a wider variety of schools drew increased governmental attention and public debate. The expectation that the public schools would solve all manner of social problems increased, as did the feeling among some that public schools were intruding too far into matters of family privacy and belief. Schooling problems began to look astronomical.

The force of gravity exerted by mainstream culture in the sixties and seventies did not grow at a pace equal to the growth of expectations for public schools. More and more people expected public schools to solve social and cultural problems while fewer and fewer people had faith that the programs generated by mainstream culture would actually work. As government policy was extended through public schools, it became necessary for people to confront the differences between their own consciences and what was perceived as the bureaucratized reality of majority culture in public schools. Some of these confrontations were reactionary, as in resistance to racial equality. But much of it was simply countercultural—the spinning off of families and groups to explore new value systems or religious world views through alternative communities and schools. As the field of influence of the central culture weakened, more people became "free" to be attracted by alternative beliefs and the alternative schools that embodied and tried to transmit these beliefs to children. Caught between the value systems of the majority and of the dissenters were a vast number of confused or apathetic people whose lack of strongly held values made them subject to politico-cultural manipulation. When the government increases regulation and control of private schools, it is the allegiance of these free-floating people that it is trying to gain.

Private-school regulation became more important, and as it did, the likelihood of clashes between majority and dissenting views of school and society increased. Coherent state policies did not emerge, however. In fact, the regulation of dissenting groups by public-school authorities proceeded as a spasmodic reaction to perceived threats from private schools. The details of these regulatory attempts, especially

143

those few that became full-blown public conflicts, provide important information about the viability of group dissent as expressed in schooling.

The struggle of the Amish for religious freedom and the struggle of the Santa Fe Community School for secular, ideological liberty were collective manifestations of belief at odds with the dominant ethic expressed in public schools. They have been the subjects of books describing both the values of the dissenting communities and their confrontations with state regulators.

Perhaps the most intriguing conflict between culture and subculture in the area of schooling took place in Kentucky between 1977 and 1980 and involved issues of Christian fundamentalism, racism, and the state of Kentucky's commitment to its definition of quality education.

The Kentucky Christian schools case provides a lens through which to view the treatment of group consciousness by public officials and state ideology. One may expect to see more of these kinds of battles as the transmission of values in schools begins to take on an equal importance to the development of academic skills. The Kentucky case began with a handful of students in fundamentalist schools, but it drew the attention and energy of powerful political forces from the state teachers' union to right-leaning Christian political groups before it was played out in the Kentucky Supreme Court and denied review by the U.S. Supreme Court. The story is further complicated by the background of racial discrimination in public schools against which almost any private school must be judged. This struggle for the minds of children thus partakes of issues of religion, community consciousness, racial discrimination, and the roots of right-wing politics, which seem to set the stage for the eighties.

14

The Fundamentals

The Reverend Harry Rudasill extended the ministry of his church in 1976 by opening Owensboro Christian Academy to forty students age six to sixteen. As pastor of Harvest Baptist Temple on the rural outskirts of Owensboro, Kentucky, Rudasill acted on a religious conviction that "Monday school should be no different from Sunday school" since, in his view, the separation of fundamental Christian values from academic learning is entirely artificial and contrary to the word of God.

A set of programmed learning materials entitled "Accelerated Christian Education" made it affordable for the faithful to hire a few born-again teachers to supervise individual learning of basic skills and the literal truths of the New Testament. It was, as Rudasill put it, a time for "more learning and less teaching." As school began, Rudasill could not have foreseen that he would ultimately find his religious ministry on trial in the case of *State Board for Elementary and Secondary Education* v. *Reverend C. Harry Rudasill, et al.*

Among the first students at Owensboro Christian Academy were two of the four children of Richard Herron, a

145

state trooper for whom the law of education comes not from the state but from God: "My rights come from the highest authority, God. The children are given to me by the Lord, and I will provide for them according to the Lord." The intense and disarmingly open Trooper Herron had seen the lack of discipline, the drugs, assaults, and unhealthy environment of the public schools as part of his work as an enforcer of the law of the state. Because Herron believed that the "public school will ultimately propagate kids without common decency, respect, or discipline," he refused to subject his children to the "public-school philosophy of secular humanism."

He had in part been driven to support Owensboro Christian Academy by the "deaf ears" of public-school officials to whom he had complained about unchristian values during the time his daughter had attended public schools. Herron's belief in the literal and inerrant truth of the Bible was thwarted by the public school, and this frustration was aggravated by his powerlessness to bring about any change that would result in the public school's reflecting his values. Owensboro Christian Academy, on the other hand, was small, seemed to increase his influence over his children, and surrounded them with other children whose families shared the same beliefs. At that time Herron did not know that he would have to engage in civil disobedience in order to preserve the community he was helping to build.

Harry Rudasill's decision to establish a Christian school as part of the mission of the church and Richard Herron's decision to send his children to that school as part of a commitment to build a religious community were being repeated all over Kentucky in the late seventies, or so the state education authorities feared. One pastor in the eastern part of the state described the mushrooming of Christian schools and religious witness among church groups as symptomatic of an "overnight awareness of moral decline" in society, which "could be seen most clearly in the public schools." Whatever the deeper dissatisfactions and aspirations of the families that joined this movement, they believed that the influence of Christianity as they understood it would insulate their children from frightening and confusing changes in the public schools.

For some fundamentalists the concern about drugs, homosexuality, permissiveness, lack of respect for authority, moral relativism, and violence became a basis for discussing larger issues of child rearing, culture, and personal disorientation. Under the surface of what might be considered a common and mundane set of complaints about schooling lay the conviction that fundamentalist religious values were the ones that might explain their world, define their future, and replace a sense of alienation with a sense of purpose and belonging.

As he speculated about what his life would be like in twenty-five years, Richard Herron vacillated between the prediction that the nation would "recover its moral fibre" by becoming less tolerant of aberrant behavior and the fear that we would "degenerate to a debased and nonfunctional condition" as the present path indicated. One thing, however, remained clear: The Second Coming of Christ would occur within our lifetime.

The premillenial horrors of the New Testament were in the minds of the fundamentalist school dissenters, and the moral decay they perceived in the schools was but a locally visible indication of the reality of premillenialism. Since only true Christians, those who are "saved," will survive the Last Days as described in the Book of Revelation, the Biblical prediction of the future was completely consistent with the fundamentalist view of schooling and the parental decision to pursue the "brotherhood of the saved" in Christian schools.

Neither the sense of cultural breakdown and spiritual decay nor the taking of refuge in the literal truth of the Bible is new for American fundamentalism, which traces its roots back to the last quarter of the nineteenth century. The vision of Apocalypse may have changed over the years, with the focus shifting from phenomena as global as communism to ones as local as public school, but the central themes of fundamentalism remain constant as does the willingness to attack materialism and skepticism while fleeing ambiguity and complexity for the solace of spiritual certainty. In the late seventies the parents of about five thousand Kentucky children, with the interpretive aid of their pastors, choose Christian schools because that is what the Bible commands and because the promise of a community of faith seemed such a clear counterweight to the self-consuming skepticism of modern thought. The Reverend Guy Goodell, one of the plaintiffs in the suit fundamentalists ultimately had to file to insulate their schools from state regulation, described the importance of Christian schools this way:

> . . . the Church is now being required to reassume the God-given responsibilities it was charged with during the Apostle Paul's day . . . We have learned that preaching, while it is at the heart of the Church, is not the Church's only responsibility. The preaching and soulwinning must always be kept central, but the social and educational ministries must not be ignored. Pure religion results from pure doctrine, and the fundamentalist will never find that in government schools.

What the fundamentalist *will* find in the public schools, according to pastors, parishioners, and parents is a variety of beliefs and behaviors that contradict the teachings of the Bible and reflect the "religion" of secular humanism. Public schools do not teach that God created the earth and all the life on it in six days or that the age of the earth is about ten thousand years. Public-school teachers are not required to be born-again Christians and tend to be tolerant of moral relativism, social complexity, and ethical ambivalence. To the fundamentalist, school authorities offer a bewildering overabundance of intellectual choices to students; to them this gives the impression that children and not adults control education. The students' attitude that "anything goes" is tolerated by public employees. The child is spoiled and the rod is spared. Public schools, according to psychologist Paul Schmidt, are much less dogmatic and much less restrictive about what they believe is okay to do with sex, drugs, alcohol and things like this. And finally, the lack of respect for civil authority . . . becomes a stronger and stronger influence. The adolescent peer group today learns not only to question but to deeply distrust civil authority such as police, judges, courtrooms, as being unfair and so a child learns this kind of negative attitude toward his government.

Dr. Schmidt, whose views proved to be very helpful to the fundamentalists in their trial, was most concerned about the negative effect of nonreligious public-school teachers as role models and authority figures: "If the child sees the teacher as someone who is not religious . . . sometimes cursing or sometimes degrading religion . . . not only does he not respect the teacher, but I have heard so many children that really fear their teachers because they feel they are involved with Satan, and you cannot learn from a teacher . . . that you feel is evil."

As in the conflict between evolution and creationism, all these criticisms of public schools are grounded in a literal reading of Scripture and regarded as the product of an anti-Christian religion with man rather than God at its center. It is, in the words of one parent, "the old conflict of good against evil" that the fundamentalists are waging. The enemy is a government-approved philosophy that places self above Scripture, narcissism above piety, and the material above the spiritual.

While the fundamentalist critics of public schooling share very few premises with Christopher Lasch, author of *The Culture of Narcissism*, they reach startlingly similar conclusions. Lasch's lament is that "institutions of cultural transmission, which might have been expected to counter the narcissistic trend of our culture (school, church, family), have instead been shaped in its image." Guy Goodell expresses a parallel view of the Last Days of the public school in a commitment to "pray, encourage, instruct, and support those who must yet face the fiery furnace of the government for failure to worship the golden image of Humanism."

149

This passionate opposition to public schools cannot be separated from the equally intense commitment to the creation of culture based upon religious conviction. In the words of one mother, "We couldn't do without reading the word of God to know what to do each day."

Christian schools in Kentucky are viewed by families and pastors alike as places in which there is no separation of religious values from learning the skills needed to function in society. The old distinction between secular and sectarian learning, which the Catholic hierarchy once urged upon the courts as a means of securing state aid without violating the separation of church and state, is rejected by fundamentalists. The teaching function of the school is part of the general ministry of the fundamentalist church to win souls for Christ and to act as a Christian brotherhood in the midst of chaos and decay. Ministers are often teachers in the schools. Others who teach are often required to be born-again Christians so that they provide the role models the church desires. Even the word "church" refers to the community of the faithful, with words like "temple" and "auditorium" being used to describe the church building. Within the church community the school functions to "take the child at the very youngest age and begin to provide the teaching, inculcating of the Bible doctrine in his heart and mind at that age." Critical thinking is not the aim of Christian schooling.

The transmission of religious values through schooling and other ministries serves to maintain a faith community that cannot rely for its cohesion on being geographically localized or contained. "To prohibit or to prevent any future difficulties in the lives of children growing up we need to have some type of ministry to them in obedience to Bible command," as one pastor put it. The attempt to infuse religious values as understood by fundamentalists includes the prescription of an entire "lifestyle" in school and in the public and private lives of parishioners. This lifestyle covers everything from hair length for males to the hierarchy of obedience and a prohibition of drinking, all of which are said to be drawn from a literal interpretation of the Bible.

If the schools do not recognize a separation of secular and religious activities and if pastors insist upon the oneness of school and faith community, unity is not the word to describe the relationship of the fundamentalist community to the society at large. Separation of the faithful from society is the goal. Many fundamentalist schools will not admit children of parents who are not saved. Some will not even engage in sports contests with schools whose students are tainted by humanistic beliefs. The effort is to reduce the dissonance between their religious beliefs and the worldly reality, which appears so chaotic and evil to them. The process of separation into believers' churches, which has been accelerating since the early sixties, is alleged to have its roots in ancient times.

Professor George Williams, a theologian and church historian at Harvard who was an expert witness for the fundamentalists in the 1978 trial, described these separatist roots:

> . . . plaintiffs are very much like the early Christians who expressed it in the community of faith which separates itself from the surrounding community. Christians were in the pre-Constantinian age repellant to a great many of the magistrates of the Roman Empire because they withdrew for their own religious and moral purposes into gatherings, conventicles, in which the education was carried on by the bishop who would also be called the pastor. So that these people have a precedent in Christian antiquity regarding the church, the homes from which the children come, church edifice, the past, and the friends and older people, their peers as the community to which they belong and from whom they gain that knowledge which makes it possible for them to swear allegiance to Christ as sovereign in their lives.

> (Transcript: *State Board* v. *Rudasill*)

The political history of fundamentalism in the United States, from the prosecution of biology teachers like John Scopes and the creation of Prohibition to the electronic preachers of the Moral Majority, is, of course, testimony to the inconsistency of separationist doctrine among fundamentalists. Even the most pious of believers do not extend the doctrine of separation to their economic livelihoods; and unlike the totally separatist Amish, it is the rare fundamentalist who will shun politics or refuse to utilize the courts of the wider society to gain his own ends. Nevertheless, there is a clear sense of isolation among the Kentucky fundamentalists whose deep religious convictions prompt them to participate in Christian fundamentalist schools. Harry Rudasill observed that "few parents will sacrifice popularity, money, and the so-called benefits of public education just to see that their children get a Christian education. We know we are moral, but in spite of Jerry Falwell, we know we are not a majority."

There is a temptation to write off the sincerity of fundamentalist belief in separatism and therefore to discount their commitment to a Biblical community of faith. But the lives of many of these people do clearly bear witness to the depth of their convictions. The historical connection between grass-roots fundamentalism and right-wing politics may prove only that fundamentalist politicians, like their counterparts in other quarters, are not above exploiting the needs and beliefs of the people from whom they can draw political strength.

In conversation and testimony, families who describe the strength of Christian schools return again and again to value and belief issues. Basic skills, like reading or arithmetic, are important but secondary to the problems of establishing a moral and religious atmosphere and socializing children in these values. It is the absence of this atmosphere from public schools that is so readily attacked. The public schools might be trusted to teach reading but cannot be trusted to enforce morality.

Repeated references to drug problems, homosexuality, lack of discipline, and the absence of respected authority in public schools do not so much express an assessment that these problems are widespread, as a fear that there is no recognizable moral fabric in public schools and that the schools have forsaken their once clear mission of socializing children into moral, Christian adults. This desire for clear and understandable values is part of the search for a cultural fabric capable of binding together diverse aspects of daily life. The problem of schooling children is a microcosm of the problem of adult living, and what the families find missing from public schools, they find present in Christian schools—a cohesiveness or sense of shared beliefs that is absent from American life. The rhetoric of schooling and the language of religion come to focus upon the central felt need for order expressed in shared values and assumptions.

The search for community, which is reflected in decisions to send children to fundamentalist Christian schools, is made more urgent by the lack of influence these people feel over public schools. In most areas they are prevented by law and politics from establishing their religious values in public schools, and their attempts to inject morality through demands for nonreligious discipline have often been dismissed out of hand by public-school officials.

The conclusion being drawn is that individual political activity does not yield results. Here, the families are seeing only the tip of a potentially deep contradiction in their beliefs. Fundamentalism is deeply individualistic. Individual salvation is the cornerstone of the fundamentalist church, and pastors repeatedly reaffirm the responsibility of parents to make educational decisions. But the ability of individual parents to influence schooling is clearly less than the collective ability of the church controlled by the pastor.

The Christian schools are created and are successful and are sought after because they provide collective support and sustain shared beliefs. Like the seventeenth-century Puritans of Massachusetts Bay, the fundamentalists are compelled to operate on a collective, organized, and sometimes hierarchical basis, which seems to be at odds with their individualist theology. The strengthening of the faith community, partly through schooling, becomes an important element in sustaining individual religious freedom. In turn, the defense of community becomes the uncomfortable tactic of individualists who roundly condemn socialism and collectivism as "basic and necessary to tyranny."

This ambivalence about the collective and the individual is reflected in the fundamentalist attitude toward freedom of belief, especially in the schools. For over fifty years fundamentalists have been a driving force behind intolerance and narrow-mindedness, and Christian schools are not wellsprings of intellectual emancipation.

If the Bible said the world was flat, that would undoubtedly be a part of the fundamentalist curriculum; yet when the state education authority seeks to regulate the standards of Christian schools, fundamentalists wish only to be left in peace to develop their own subculture and pass it on to their children. This switching of attitudes is more than merely the use of arguments of convenience, which is so prevalent in public debate everywhere.

The fluctuation between tolerance and intolerance or between individualism and collectivism or between spirituality and materialism all reflect a consciousness caught between two cultures. At the same time a community of faith is being built around the literal interpretation of ancient Scripture, the attractiveness and utility of the secular, statist, and bureaucratized culture of narcissism cannot be denied. The issues about which the fundamentalists are ambivalent are among the deepest issues for American consciousness. Their search for a stable, religiously based subculture and for the educational means of sustaining it is an effort to resolve these issues and institutionalize the resulting world view.

Looking to schools to reinforce and help define the community of the faithful does not distinguish Kentucky's fundamentalist Christians from their secular or liberal brethren or from the supporters of public schooling. Acculturation

154

and social improvement have been staples of American school ideology for so long that the Supreme Court has begun to count them among the assumptions of which it takes notice without requiring proof. Scratch the surface of the public-school criticism of Christian fundamentalist schools in Kentucky and you find not a concern for critical thought and open minds but a fear that unacceptable values are being inculcated.

In the 1920's Jesse Stuart, one of Kentucky's most noted and able writers, put this faith in the curative powers of schooling this way:

> The schoolroom was the gateway to all problems of humanity. It was the gateway to the correcting of evils. It was the gateway to inspire the nation's succeeding generations to greater and more beautiful living with each other; to happiness, to health, to brotherhood, to everything!

Stuart sought to spread a separate gospel from that adhered to by fundamentalists, then and now. He believed deeply and preached forcefully, as witness his success as a Kentucky public-school teacher. He shared with the fundamentalists not specific beliefs and world views but a sense of urgency in gaining adherents and building a group of converts whose very existence seemed proof of the worth of specific beliefs.

The Christian fundamentalists of Kentucky, as distinguished from their political leaders and electronic preachers, are deeply religious, spiritual, and often antimaterialistic people; nevertheless, there is a hard edge to their spirituality, an overzealous proselytizing that seems to put intolerance of differing beliefs on a personal level. They believe they are commanded by the Bible to preach the Gospel, and so they do at every opportunity. But the tenacity and the aggressiveness of this preaching is often so intense that it appears to lose depth and subtlety and become a wooden recitation of a formula for personal security. Certainly, it does not invite tolerance in return.

155

It is perceivable that the fundamentalists have been touched by the depth and universality of the Bible and have absorbed some of its spiritual, even mystical nature; yet, at the same time, they appear to be thinking mechanically, to be clinging to rules without admitting the possibility of interpretation. It sometimes sounds as if they were convincing themselves, rather than their listeners, of the validity of their views. It's almost as if they suspected that these incantations of belief were the last life boat in a sea of collapsed meanings and that the boat had sprung a fatal leak.

The establishment and attractiveness of the approximately fifty Christian schools in Kentucky in the late seventies represented the acting out of all the ambivalences and contradictions of people searching for a sense of belonging and of meaning through the establishment of a community of belief. For this fragile subculture the struggle against state regulation or any other enemy is necessary to the group's self-definition. Christian schools were created in response to the perceived decline of order in the culture at large. Defending these schools and asserting the existence of the brotherhood of the faithful helps to bring that brotherhood into existence. The Christian schools of Kentucky are a manifestation of a more generalized search for legitimate authority.

15
The Devil's Advocate

When the Kentucky State Board of Education began imposing regulations on Christian schools in 1977, fundamentalists regarded the action as an attempt to make their schools reject the Bible in favor of secular humanism. "If the state tells us what kinds of textbooks to have," the pastor and principal of Clays Mill Christian Academy in Lexington asked, "what do we have? A glorified public school." This was not the kind of glory the Reverend T. Eugene Holmes had in mind when he refused to seek accreditation and rejected state standards. "We try to gauge [our school] to meet God's standards for education," he said.

The laws of Kentucky provide for the annual accreditation of schools by the State Department of Education, an obligation state officials interpreted to include private as well as public schools. The standards for accreditation adopted by the state and revised in June of 1976 set out a complex set of requirements for being classified as "comprehensive, standard, basic, provisional, or special." Those schools without any state classification were unapproved.

Until the summer of 1977 state officials had not sought to impose these standards upon private schools, though some Catholic parochial schools and even a few older fundamentalist schools had sought, and received, approval. Then in August the state board ordered local public-school officials to begin enforcing the truancy laws against parents whose children attended unaccredited private schools. This was done in spite of the fact that the same board had made no substantial effort to deal with the thousands of truants who attended neither private nor public schools.

The implication of the board's sudden interest in rigorous enforcement of accreditation standards and truancy laws against fundamentalists was that the board felt it had the power not only to judge the quality of schools in the state but to determine which schools should exist.

In September local public school officials, under orders from the state, began informing the parents of children attending unaccredited fundamentalist schools such as Owensboro Christian Academy and Clays Mill Christian Academy that their children would be considered truant. Individual Christian schools, along with the Kentucky Association of Christian Schools, sought to delay the enforcement of state standards while they raised legal questions about the standards' legality. Turning these appeals for further consideration aside, the state escalated the conflict by threatening to bring actions against the principals and teachers of some of the schools for "unlawful transaction with a minor," a misdemeanor consisting of inducing or causing a minor to become an "habitual truant." The charges would have had the effect of closing down the schools and subjecting the offenders to up to a year's imprisonment.

The Christian schools banded together and hired both local and out-of-state counsel and attempted to negotiate a compromise rather than begin litigation. But the state hardened its stand by announcing that unless certain schools were closed unlawful transaction charges would be filed.

The fundamentalists began preparing for a fight. On a Friday in mid-September, the parents of Owensboro Christian Academy and others were informed by certified letter that unless they enrolled their children in accredited schools by the following Monday, they would face legal action. During that weekend Trooper Richard Herron, who had no intention of trusting his children's education to anyone other than the Reverend Harry Rudasill, borrowed a light plane and flew attorneys for the Christian schools all around the state to collect from parents and pastors the affidavits necessary to mount a legal challenge to the state's enforcement of accreditation standards. Monday morning the people who were to become plaintiffs in *State Board of Elementary and Secondary Education* v. *Rudasill* obtained a temporary restraining order from state Circuit Court Judge Henry Meigs, halting the enforcement of truancy laws against them and preventing state interference with the operation of the unaccredited religious schools.

Preparations for the full-blown legal conflict occupied several months; and it was not until June of 1978 that the trial was held. It was October of 1978 before the circuit court ruled against the state and October of 1979 before the state supreme court unanimously affirmed that compulsory schooling could be "required in order to prepare children . . . to intelligently participate as citizens in a democracy but not to uniformly develop them socially and morally in the same educational mold." The state board, which had begun by trying to eliminate schools of which it did not approve, ended by being denied the legal power to impose any substantive regulations on any nonpublic schools.

The fundamentalist Christian schools did not object to the requirements set forth in the Kentucky statutes. Their difficulty was with the standards the state board claimed to have adopted pursuant to those statutes. As required by the legislature, the schools in question taught in English; offered instruction in the branches of learning required by law; complied with the law on number of days and hours of operation, health, safety and fire standards, and immunization. They were willing to make available to the state the results of standardized achievement tests as evidence of their students' accomplishments.

When the source of requirements moved beyond the legislature to the state board, however, the Christian schools felt their mission was being jeopardized. The religious schools objected to being required to use state-approved textbooks and to hire only state-certified teachers. They objected to being forced to offer a large array of courses to a small number of students, and they found *Standards for Accrediting Kentucky Schools* to be confusing, contradictory, and so arbitrary that they were unable to determine what was being required of them.

The schools and the parents of children attending them described the regulations as an effort to limit their religious freedom and undermine their faith community. The state responded that it did not seek to outlaw courses that taught the Bible. But the school had no such courses, preferring instead to integrate religion into every aspect of instruction. The state's teaching, textbook, and curriculum requirements were viewed by the private schools as dominating the field and leaving no room for their own philosophy. The state board saw itself as enforcing minimum standards that would reduce the opportunities for charlatans to start schools—a problem for the future, not a description of the present. There was no attack on the quality of the Christian fundamentalist schools. Instead, the action against them was justified by a deputy superintendent for elementary and secondary schools as a means of attaining "clarification of the law" as related to private schools.

Discovering the political and cultural agenda underlying the state's sudden and intense interest in regulating the private schools of Christian Fundamentalists will always be partly speculative. The Reverend Bob Brown, a free-thinking Baptist minister who chaired the state Board of Education during part of the conflict, has died. Few others will discuss such slippery matters as motivation or admit to interests that the courts have since declared illegal. Nevertheless, a consistent image of the factors that led the state to expend so much energy in trying to control such a small number of families and schools does emerge from conversations with school officials, attorneys, parents, and clergy involved with the conflict.

The abortive attempt to control nonpublic schooling in Kentucky must be seen in the context of what the state education establishment might have predicted or feared would develop in schooling in the eighties. According to the best estimates made in 1977, only around 10 percent of the state's approximately 650,000 school-age children attended private schools, and of these, a mere 5,000 were enrolled in fundamentalist Christian academies. Elite private schools and Catholic parochial schools remained stable in size and accepted state regulation. But Christian schools were growing in Kentucky as elsewhere faster than mushrooms after a rainstorm. The outlook for government-operated schools was not promising since both budgets and birth rates were declining. But although resources would become more scarce, a sizeable education establishment had been created and required support.

The quality of Kentucky's public schools and the working conditions they provided for teachers had come a long way since the twenties. It was then that Jesse Stuart made fifty dollars a month in a one-room school where some of his twenty-year-old first-grade pupils would as soon have beaten him up as let him teach. By the late seventies the Kentucky Teachers' Association had grown to 29,000 members and was one of the most powerful political forces in the entire state. With all these developments in mind, the rapid, unchecked growth of totally private schools that celebrated the "old time religion" could easily have been seen as the leading edge of an attack on the public-school domain.

Teaching jobs, bargaining power, working conditions, financial resources, and an administrative structure were all on the line in the battle over state regulation of private schools. Kentucky, like other states, today pays a per capita amount to local school districts based on their average daily attendance. Public service radio announcements aired in 1981 urged parents to be sure their children were at the local public school in October when the census was to be taken because each absent child would cost the public schools $7.50 per day in state aid. According to the ad, parents could help to purchase the supplies and pay the teachers their children would need just by sending them to the public school regularly.

If the estimate of the Kentucky Association of Christian Schools is accurate and there are 5,000 students willing to admit their presence in fundamentalist schools, the loss to the local school districts would be 6.5 million dollars for a 180-day school year. The fundamentalist schools make no claim on this money and would not accept it if it were offered. But the loss to the public-school treasury is not insignificant. If the trend in growth of Christian schools continues and the absence of regulations permits the continued siphoning off of students to nongovernment schools, the ability of public-school finances to support the structure of personnel it has built up will be severely weakened.

The same projected growth would increase the number of noncertified teachers who would not be inclined to bargain collectively and would be exempt from National Labor Relations Review Board supervision on religious grounds. The result would be not only a loss of union influence over salaries but the decline of what one teacher called "enlightened, nonparochial, and professionally open working conditions." The rights, privileges, and conditions of teaching, which the profession had struggled to create, were already under attack by religious zealots and conservative budget cutters. Several people close to the school regulation conflict suggested that the Kentucky Education Association (KEA) and the state board had closely allied interests in bringing the Christian schools under control. One former teacher suggested that in addition to the obvious financial pressures in favor of regulation, there was also a valid fear of an unknown subculture in the teaching profession. The conditions of teaching had become so professionalized, she implied, that available jobs might be given to people whose values were unprofessional and even antiprofessional. Teachers had their professional standards as well as their salaries at risk.

This sense of professionalism accounts in part for the secondary interest of the state in regulating private schools: resisting an attack on public-school competence. The Reverend Harry Rudasill, the pastor and principal of the Owensboro Christian Academy, illustrated the board's defensiveness with an anecdote: He had a visit from a member of the state Board of Education one year after the school opened. Rudasill had been responding to state inquiries out of courtesy when he was abruptly told that he could not use the Accelerated Christian Education materials, which constituted a kind of individualized programmed learning. The visiting board member discussed the materials with Rudasill and took his insistence on using these religious materials as a personal insult, claiming, "I have been a schoolteacher and I know you cannot achieve your goal by this method." Just at that time a first grader was passing the pastor's office and was invited in to read from a sixth-grade reader. He did so fluently, and the board member left in a huff. Professional educators do not like to hear laymen claim that they can do as good a job as government-approved teachers.

More provocative still were the direct criticisms of the public schools made by fundamentalists. No public-school official felt threatened by being attacked for failing to teach that all life was created in six days. But the schools and school personnel were vulnerable to accusations about high-school drug culture, violence, drinking, and lack of discipline in the public schools. According to one state education official, "As the majority of the population gets to be over sixty-five, rather than of school age, they relate to what happened when they were in school." The result of this somewhat dated understanding of public-school life is that the public is hypersensitive to criticisms, which in fact reflect only a small portion of public-school reality and that the public-school officials "have no pipeline to their audience." These same criticisms later served to undercut the state's position as a regulator of private schools in which no such unseemly behavior was tolerated.

Beneath the vulnerability of exaggerated criticism, public-school officials also feared that the prophesies of moral decay might become self-fulfilling. The possibility was perceived, though not openly discussed, that the Christian schools might increasingly draw off the most motivated and stable students, leaving the public schools with a still greater proportion of the problems of education. Left with declining resources and stripped of flexibility by the very regulations they sought to impose upon private schools, public-school officials feared they might find themselves incapable of providing a quality of education high enough to fend off the fundamentalist attack.

The central factor that accounted for the excessive control of private schools attempted by the state of Kentucky was not potential financial or professional losses but ideological warfare. The Christian schools and the public schools did not share a philosophy of how to deal with children or of what constitutes reality, the basis of knowledge, the nature of learning, or the meaning of life. In brief, the two camps did not share the same culture. What they did agree upon was that the central function of schooling is acculturation.

Each side felt its own vision of life and learning was so correct that it defined the best interests of children and society. These competing visions were not subject to rational justification or compromise. They constituted the reference points of personal identity. The contest over teacher certification and textbook requirements was, at bottom, a battle for the minds of children. Regulation and resistance were efforts by competing ideologies to capture the consciousness of those who, upon becoming adults, would influence the shape of society and the distribution of its material benefits. Of course all of this had to be played out under the cover of educational jargon on the one side and the Bible on the other, because neither side could admit the bias inherent in its position that children are but potential converts to the one right way.

In spite of the inevitability of schooling as acculturation, those who were out of power had the luxury of appearing to be fighting for freedom without having to discuss the authoritarian nature of their schools or the illusions inherent in their religious convictions. The state, which was equally interested in consciousness manipulation, had to bear the burden of justifying an exercise of power over the beliefs of private citizens while defending the inadequacies of its own educational and social philosophy. The state seemed to be revealed as ineptly authoritarian while the fundamentalists were freedom-loving libertarians. But as former Governor and Federal Appeals Court Judge Bert Combs stated in assessing his defense of the state's case, "The arbitrary power of the pastor in these schools and churches is unlike anything the U.S. Constitution would permit in a public institution." It was never possible for the public to see the issue as a power conflict between two equally authoritarian ideologies.

The one strength in the state's position was never developed. It remained a background factor that might have been considered by the state Board of Education or been the subject of regulation or been brought up at the trial to justify the state's regulatory efforts. In the end, the relationship of private schooling to racism remained the issue that no one wanted to examine openly but everyone was willing to speculate about. It clearly was a factor in the state's actions but not in the way state officials would have liked to believe.

In 1975 in the state's largest city, Louisville, a federal court order was entered requiring the desegregation of public schools in Jefferson County and establishing a program of busing as part of ending the victimization of black pupils by government schools. The "white flight," which resulted from resistance to the desegregation plan, reached 10,000 pupils in the eighteen months before the situation stabilized. The city's Catholic bishop refused to open the doors of parochial schools to those families whose primary motivation for religious education was to avoid sending their children to school with nonwhites. Most of the whites who left the city's public schools moved just across the Ohio River to rural counties in Kentucky or southern Indiana.

It was very shortly after the beginning of desegregation busing that the growth of Christian fundamentalist schools began to increase around the state. The suspicion thus arose that the mushrooming of Christian schools and the resistance to desegregation might be indistinguishable in their effects, if not in their motivations; yet no complaints of discriminatory admissions policies were filed, and the pastoral claims of unbiased policies went unchallenged except by innuendo.

A few private schools, dedicated to the preservation of racism and cloaked in the sacred garb of Christian piety, did emerge in response to school desegregation, but the state did not choose to make a test case out of them. Judge Combs observed that by the time he had entered the case for the state, the die was already cast, for none of the fundamentalist schools involved had demonstrably discriminatory policies. In fact, few of the Christian schools in existence at the time of the regulation conflict were in Louisville. Most were in rural, predominantly white areas.

One school that was in Louisville, the Portland Christian Academy, had been there for over fifty years. Earl Mullins, the pastor and senior administrator of the academy, described the motivations of families attending the school as "a belief in the reality of Jesus as the son of God and a commitment to following for themselves and their children the pattern of life of Jesus Christ as set out in the New Testament."

Portland Christian, which occupies a gray cinder-block building behind the Universal Church of Christ in a rundown working class area of Louisville, has been racially integrated since 1968, according to Mullins. In 1980–1981, 10 percent of its 310 pupils were nonwhite. It was the existence of a school like Portland Christian and the absence of evidence that other schools were interfering significantly with the desegregation process that led the attorney for the plain-

166

tiffs in the desegregation suit to conclude that intervention against the Christian schools was pointless. In fact, Harry Rudasill's attorney, Tom Hogan, brought the matter to the Kentucky Civil Liberties Union to see if their board would support the religious schools.

Given facts like these, Combs chose to "give them the benefit of the doubt." He didn't feel he could get the evidence to substantiate an argument (based on race) that the state board had compelling interests to protect in regulating private schools. Why the state board failed to initiate prosecutions of clearly racist private schools and went after the more religiously sincere and racially open Christian schools instead remains a mystery. One of the attorneys for the Christian fundamentalist schools acknowledges that they probably would have lost their case if the state had pursued racist schools first.

One solution to the mystery is obvious. In the judgment of some political observers in Kentucky, the state Board of Education could not have afforded politically to take a stand against racism while some members of the public were so vocally resistant to school desegregation.

The fundamentalist schools that were under attack by the state also showed a reluctance to confront the issue of race. The Owensboro Christian Academy, for example, is all white, and its pastor, Harry Rudasill, is troubled by the absence of black children from a school he very convincingly states "originated from conviction, not white flight." He acknowledges the legitimacy of a state regulatory concern for white flight in Louisville; yet Rudasill makes no effort to recruit a variety of students and in fact has hired one of the same attorneys who helped defend his religious liberty to help him resist the demand of the Internal Revenue Service that a recruitment plan for minority students and staff be instituted at the school. The same schools and attorneys and associations that fought so valiantly for their own freedom of belief and association joined the battle in Washington, D.C., to prevent the IRS from denying tax exemptions to private schools that practice racial discrimination. There is no evidence of racism in most of the Christian schools, but neither is there any evidence that they cared about the racial consequences of pursuing their own personal interests.

The issue is not the sincerity of the religious beliefs of the Christian schools or the inability of the state education establishment to protect the educational freedom of its citizens, regardless of race. The issue is not the racial motives or intentions of Christian school operators, parents, or state bureaucrats. American society has racism too well ingrained in its institutional structure for the analysis of racial inequality to be confined to the search for individual racists and racist intentions. Since racism exists all by itself, without the aid of evil individuals and purposeful discrimination, the issue must be the effect that any political or legal struggle has upon racist conditions.

The failure of the state of Kentucky to prosecute segregationist academies prior to legitimate Christian schools, its failure to add to its myriad regulations a prohibition of racial discrimination in approved private schools, its unwillingness to search for evidence of private discrimination or to raise the issue forcefully at trial all add up to a policy of not so benign neglect. This is also the tally for the actions of the Christian schools that went to the trouble of affirming their belief in racial equality at the trial but did not see it as part of their Christian mission to consider the effect of their pursuit of liberty on the liberty of racial minorities. It is hard to credit either the Christian claim to religious liberty or the state interest in preventing racial discrimination as being totally honorable. Clearly, it was not the intention of any of the parties to the regulation struggle to foster or condone racism. But while their sincerity is unimpeachable, the strength of their commitment to racial equality and their ability to analyze the consequences of their actions leave much to be desired. Had the two sides had the same courage of their convictions in matters of race as they had in other matters of consciousness manipulation, the outcome of the conflict would have been different. Perhaps all that can be said of the concern of the state board and the Christian schools for institutional racism in Kentucky is contained in the slogan, "If you ain't part of the solution, you're part of the problem."

In order to protect its financial and professional power as well as fend off an attack against public schools and win the battle for the minds of children, the state Board of Education had chosen to attack Christian fundamentalist schools. As June of 1978 approached, the state was faced with a trial in which the claim of religious liberty would obliterate all these concerns and drastically cut the power of the public-school establishment to impose its acculturation process upon dissenting communities of belief.

16

The Trial, the Appeal, and the Last Judgment

However contradictory, literal-minded, or just plain wrong-headed Christian fundamentalist views may seem, they do constitute a set of sincerely held beliefs about the meaning and proper conduct of life. William B. Ball, one of the nation's leading constitutional trial lawyers, was able to use these beliefs to turn a skirmish over the approval of textbooks and teachers into a full-scale battle over the highest of constitutional principles: religious freedom. With the consummate skill bred of extensive experience and personal commitment to liberty, Ball structured the case, defined the issues, used expert testimony, embarrassed the opposition, and took advantage of their errors. In Ball's hands, *State Board* v. *Rudasill* moved out of the realm of ambivalent motives and the fragile sense of community onto the plane of clear constitutional commands. The state, in the words of one of its chief attorneys, "was out-lawyered."

The crucial element of the fundamentalists' trial strategy was to use the legal framework the Supreme Court had adopted in exempting the Amish of Wisconsin from that state's compulsory education law. Ball had handled that case as well, and he knew the kind of evidence that would be capable of sustaining a positive decision all the way to the high court. The Yoder case had had four basic elements: One, the Amish were puritanical, law-abiding, and non-threatening to mainstream American culture; two, the Amish constituted a religious community, which adhered to a doctrine of separation from wordly matters; three, the ties that bound the Amish community were religious beliefs that infused every aspect of their lives and whose sincerity and centrality had been attested to by centuries of practice; and four, the clash between the beliefs and values of Amish life and those inculcated in public schools created an alienating and destructive tension in the minds of Amish children, threatening the viability of their community.

These were rather narrow categories in which to fit a subculture seeking to preserve its freedom of acculturation, and Ball must have been nagged by the memory of Chief Justice Burger's words in 1972 that "it cannot be overemphasized that we are not dealing with a way of life and mode of education by a group claiming to have recently discovered some 'progressive' or more enlightened process for rearing children for modern life."

The crux of the fundamentalist schools' case against the state Board of Education was that the state's regulations amounted to an attempt to supervise and control private Christian schools and violated the right of religious freedom of the fundamentalist families. The trial transcript is laced with evidence that suggests that the families claiming this right are model Americans. Although the legal theory of religious liberty is not based on judgments about the moral character of those who assert their freedom, the plaintiffs' attorneys knew they had to put some distance between their clients and the various fringe cults that were evoking public horror at the time.

A clinical psychologist who testified for the plaintiffs offered as his expert opinion the contention that it was the public schools that fostered "lack of respect for civil authority" and the Christian academies that had "a reverence for the government and government authorities." The byword of Christian education was claimed to be "discipline," including a rigid hierarchy of authority within the family and school and the spanking of unruly children "in a way that leaves the child with a good deal of self-respect." Only when civil law is contradicted by the Word of God, as in the regulation of Christian education by humanists, need it be feared that fundamentalists would engage in civil disobedience.

The authoritarian and law-abiding nature of Christian belief and practice was reinforced by the testimony of Richard Herron, the embodiment of the civil law enforcer turned disobedient. Herron testified about a list of criminal offenses perpetrated by children in public schools, from rape and theft to arson and drug abuse. He had seen none of this sort of activity in Christian schools. And finally, in addition to the testimony of pastors and parents about the basically puritanical lifestyle of fundamentalists, the plaintiffs produced the expert testimony of Dr. Rousas John Rushdoony. Rushdoony, a Presbyterian minister and theologian, described the historical roots of fundamentalism in early Christian experience and stated that "contemporary fundamentalism is very strictly law-abiding, regards it as a religious principle, but believes that we must obey God rather than man as Saint Peter declared . . . where the state demands something contrary to the requirements of Scripture."

Any judge or member of the public watching this trial could hardly have entertained the fear that what was being taught in Christian schools was antiauthoritarian, antiestablishment, progressive, antihierarchic, freewheeling, or in any way a threat to the central tenets of a bureaucratic and statist culture. The impression was left that Christian schools were simply doing what public schools ought to have been doing: turning out God-fearing patriots who know the importance of traditional values.

The plaintiffs had somewhat more difficulty analogizing themselves to the victorious Amish of *Yoder* v. *Wisconsin* when it came to demonstrating a religious community separate from the world. But the testimony of experts, so well orchestrated by William Ball throughout the trial, proved sufficient. Among the eighty-one Findings of Fact the trial judge made in his October 1978 decision was one that stated: "The attitude, support, example, and lifestyle of a child's teachers and peers, and the school's environment, philosophy, and textbooks, are critical in the moral development of the child's acceptance, assimilation, and acquisition of religious beliefs and convictions."

Another finding determined that "the schools are of critical importance in the integration of children into the fundamentalist Christian faith community."

The "faith community" was acknowledged by plaintiffs not to be totally separate and self-sufficient. It is instead a joining of persons on the basis of belief and philosophy rather than geography and institutional structure. The Reverend Guy Goodell of the Frankfort Baptist Tabernacle testified that

> one of the primary purposes of our school is to teach the Biblical concept of separation. We believe that our church leaders, in compliance with Paul's letter to Timothy, should be separated and should follow certain guidelines . . . We are not Amish, but our separation is defined and is strong and is Biblical. For example, in John 17, Jesus, in what is called the High Priestly Prayer, emphasized that believers are in the world but not of the world . . . that we can move within the world but that we are not to take our direction of conformity from the world, such as dress standards, moral standards, cultural values, and the inculcation of principles and ideas in the community which are in conflict with the Bible.

Harvard historian and professor of theology George Williams testified that this concept of separation and faith community was historically rooted.

The fundamentalists had little trouble demonstrating by their own testimony and that of experts that their religious beliefs were sincere and infused every aspect of their lives. Religious training was shown to be totally integrated with

173

all other aspects of education rather than separated from allegedly secular activities, lending credence to the idea of a faith community. By tying these practices to those of early Christians, the fundamentalists were able to demonstrate that they were not "a group claiming to have recently discovered some . . . more enlightened process for rearing children."

The state's attorneys attempted to show that these religious values and the faith community were not encroached upon by minimum state standards for textbooks and teachers, but by this time the court was awash in references to the travails of early Christians who refused to renounce the sovereignty of Christ for that of Caesar. Judge Meigs found that the plaintiffs' religious beliefs were truly and sincerely held, that Christian schools are an integral part of church ministry, and that compliance with state regulations "would have the effect of imposing state chosen philosophical values upon plaintiffs" and "would violate the religious convictions of the plaintiffs."

Testimony of the plaintiff's expert witness in the area of child psychology provided the last necessary analogy to the Amish. Dr. Paul Schmidt described the symptoms of mental distress and inability to learn and relate to family and peers children suffer when public-school values contradict the religious beliefs of the children's fundamentalist families. An inconsistency of belief and authority between parent and school would cause a child to become angry, disrespect authority, become resentful, suffer guilt and even blame himself, become depressed, lose motivation for study and life, and, in extreme cases, "wind up punishing himself for not being what he thinks he should be, with wrist-slashing, the ultimate being suicide."

Children were thus the ultimate victims of the state's insistence that Christian schools should be operated contrary to the religious beliefs of the faith community that established those schools. The process of acculturation would be interrupted and even destroyed with the result being the ultimate demise of the community and destruction of its beliefs.

In the two full days of testimony by experts and laymen, the plaintiffs had succeeded in making religious freedom the central issue in the case and in demonstrating that state regulation of Christian schools would destroy a nonthreatening, separatist faith community by destroying its means of perpetuating beliefs among its members' children.

Some of those involved in the case on the state's side did not believe that minimum academic standards would encroach upon the ability of the Christian schools to inculcate religious values. Former Governor Combs, who represented the state at the trial, observed in hindsight that the issue of religious freedom had become a fixation of Americans recently and that "everyone is for religious freedom in Kentucky." But Combs could not find anything in the trial record to show that religious freedom was actually curtailed by the state regulations and viewed the issue as not really related to the facts of the case. "We don't need a straw man to show how dedicated we are to religious liberty," he said.

Whether religious liberty was a straw man created by a crafty attorney to engage the righteous indignation of the court or was a fundamental issue of central importance to the lives of the plaintiffs, it carried the case. Judge Meigs followed his eighty-one Findings of Fact with a ruling that the textbook and teacher certification requirements of the state violated the Free Exercise Clause of the First Amendment, the Establishment Clause of the First Amendment, and Section Five of the Kentucky constitution, which reads in part, "Nor shall any man be compelled to send his child to any school he may in conscience oppose." The inability of the state to resist the religious characterization of the facts was in large part attributable to the inadequacy of the regulations it was defending. Kentucky officials could not convincingly claim to be insuring that all students would receive at least the minimum education necessary to function as citizens of the state.

By a series of artful examinations the plaintiffs' attorneys had been able to show that the accreditation regulations were so confusing, contradictory, and laced with incomprehensible jargon and garbled syntax that even the state's own education officials could not interpret them. Neither the prevention of educational charlatanism nor the provision of due process could be served by the discretionary imposition of such gobbledegook.

But the master stroke was in expert testimony showing that the state of the literature in education research is such that no one could say with authority that the regulations would have any effect at all on the quality of education.

Professor Donald Erickson, then of the University of San Francisco School of Education, demonstrated that the profession of education knows as little about the effects of various philosophies of education as the readers of tea leaves know about the future. Erickson testified that "we do not know enough about the process [by which educational products are produced] to dictate to people as to the way in which they must run a school to produce good results." And summing up his reaction after studying the state's accreditation standards, Erickson stated, "I see no connection between these regulations and quality schooling . . . It worries me, your honor, that educators would write these things as if they were connected with educational quality."

The state had lost what might have been its most compelling argument: that it was insuring that children would not be subjected to education that would hobble them intellectually and leave them unable to function as members of a democratic society. The inadequacy of the state's standards and their intellectual indefensibility was a product of the overprofessionalization of education and left the imposition of majority culture as the only remaining justification for state regulation of religious schools.

Judge Meigs's opinion was appealed by the state directly to the Kentucky Supreme Court. In October of 1979 that court unanimously affirmed the ruling that the state could not legally impose textbook, teacher certification, or curriculum standards upon private schools. Those requirements the state could enforce included health, safety, and fire regulations; the minimum standards of course offerings and days of school required per year set out in state statutes; and the administering of achievement tests should the legislature require them in the future. But the state supreme court did not base its opinion upon the religious freedom clauses of the Federal Constitution. Instead, it relied solely upon its interpretation of that section of the Kentucky constitution that states that no parent can be forced to send a child to a school to which the parent is in conscience opposed. In effect, the court ruled that the state of Kentucky did not have the power to regulate private schools in any area that would infringe upon the rights of conscience of families.

The shift in grounds for the ruling was significant for two reasons: one, it insured that the U.S. Supreme Court would not hear an appeal since the decision rested solely upon state grounds and not upon interpretation of federal constitutional rights; and two, it left the field open to any individual or community to operate a private school without state regulation of belief or acculturation regardless of whether the school was religiously oriented or not.

Predictably, the decision was hailed on some editorial pages as a victory for freedom of belief against the mindless power of bureaucracy and condemned in other editorials as an open invitation to education fraud and the exploitation of children by unscrupulous entrepreneurs who would play upon the naïveté and ignorance of some parents.

17
A Choice of Orthodoxies

Reduced to their essence, the struggles of Christian fundamentalist schools of Kentucky, the Santa Fe Community School, and the community schooling of the Amish all represent ordinary people trying to create or sustain some form of community cohesion and shared belief that transcends public orthodoxy. Their struggles are not just against a culture they find alienating and not set up to work for them but against a government school system that seems to be bent upon cannibalizing subcultures. The history of the relationship of the state to these schools has been one of endless harassment and threat, unnecessary and overzealous legal prosecution, and the draining of resources.

These are dissenting communities, or in some cases the first stages of dissenting communities, and their values must therefore be less than universally admired. The practices and beliefs of some of them may seem bizarre, and many withstand the light of disbelieving scrutiny no better than the prevailing culture. To make matters more difficult, not only do the dissenters reject the beliefs of the majority from whom they demand tolerance, they attack those beliefs as being responsible for the social disarray and personal dislocations to which they are so sensitive.

Amidst this cultural conflict it is sometimes difficult for the outside observer to remain aware that members of dissenting communities are in pursuit of life goals and meaning that transcend state policy and mundane concerns. For their part, the institutions (government schools) assigned the job of reproducing majority culture have acted as if majority backing in the battle for children's minds entitled them to assume the supremacy of their world view for all humanity. State regulations have been based on the puffery of educational expertise, and educators have linked the defense of their financial resources and their professional status to an ideology that strikes at the core beliefs of cultural dissenters.

School bureaucracies have exercised their power in ways inconsistent with their own charters, demonstrating that public officials often express not so much the will of the majority as the agenda of those clever enough to utilize the state mechanism for their own ends. The behavior of government officials clearly indicates a hostility toward competing ideologies and toward the formation of any community that might sustain such an ideology through its way of life. It is probable that in these conflicts the intensity of hostility also reflects the degree to which established culture has deteriorated in its ability to explain reality.

The result of these struggles over value transmission in nongovernment schools has been judicial victory for a few dissenting subcultures. Viewed in this way, the cases sketched here and others like them appear to demonstrate that the law will protect the budding subculture because the law recognizes the importance of community to the generation and expression of belief. Examined more carefully, however, these cases show the opposite. Not only has the state been uniformly hostile to subcultures prior to judicial intervention but the legal doctrine generated by this intervention will operate to defeat most other attempts at sustaining group dissent. So narrow is the definition of which subcultures' schools can qualify for legal protection from state regulation that it may be said to define the exception rather than the rule.

Most conspicuous among the elements of this narrow definition is the fact that all the subculture schools that have won the right to exist on substantive grounds rather than legal technicalities have demonstrated themselves to be authoritarian and puritanical. It has been the willingness to include obedience to authority as part of the acculturation process that has recommended these community schools to the law as safe and worthy of legal protection. As arbitrators of authority, the courts have taken no chances on legitimizing groups that do not clearly indicate they will assume the responsibility for keeping individual behavior and independent thought under control. It could hardly be any other way where it is the group rather than the individual that is seeking freedom from government controls.

Carl Jung has described the way in which the truly religious, who maintain a subjective relationship to the metaphysical, are compromised by the state and become adherents to mere "creeds" that

> . . . see themselves obliged to undertake a progressive codification of their views, doctrines, and customs and in so doing have externalized themselves to such an extent that the authentic religious element in them—the living relationship to and direct confrontation with their extramundane point of reference—has been thrust into the background.

> (Jung, *The Undiscovered Self*, 1957)

The puritanism of groups such as the Amish and the Christian fundamentalists has reduced the attractiveness of those subcultures to members of the majority who might leave the public schools if they could and has made these subcultures seem safe and unlikely to proliferate. This appeal of puritanism to the courts is paradoxical. Puritanical subcultures are not likely to become substantial in size because puritanism does not strike the public as appropriate or useful for the kaleidoscopic materialism of modern life. Nevertheless, that same value structure does seem worthy of official respect because it is the basis of an organized lifestyle with the apparent strength to reject the lure of social anonymity, fast-paced vacuity, and lack of individual responsibility to the group. Although the courts have never incorporated this standard in formal legal doctrine, they *have* granted extra freedom of belief to the subculture whose puritanism makes them admired but not attractive.

The requirement of religious affiliation or adherence to religiously defined beliefs narrows the class of subculture schools eligible for legal protection still further. Thus far, dissenting secular beliefs, no matter how sincerely held or central to a group's identity, have not moved either the courts or the education bureaucrats. The Amish may gain protection for their opposition to competitiveness and their desire to live by collectivist principles, but a counterculture commune with equally anticompetitive beliefs is unlikely to convince a court that it merits the exemption from schooling granted the Amish or the exemption from state regulations granted the fundamentalists. The difference lies in whether religious affiliation is present or not. Here is how the Supreme Court described the objections of the Amish to formal schooling:

> They object to the high school and higher education generally because the values it teaches are in marked variance with Amish values and the Amish way of life; they view secondary school education as an impermissible exposure of their children to a "worldly" influence in conflict with their beliefs. The high school tends to emphasize intellectual and scientific accomplishment, self-distinction, competitiveness, worldly success, and social life with other students. Amish society emphasizes informal learning-through-doing, a life of "goodness" rather than a life of intellect, wisdom rather than technical knowledge, community welfare rather than competition, and separation rather than integration with contemporary worldly society.

181

In spite of the fact that these same objections might be made with equal sincerity by those without religious affiliations, the Court made it plain that no escape hatch was being created for the merely "philosophical" dissenter from orthodox child-rearing practices.

In the Rudasill case itself the same theme underlies the result. Judge Combs agreed that the Kentucky Supreme Court ruling all but eliminated state power to regulate the content of private schooling. But he was equally sure that no secular private school the state tried to regulate could win its case: "The court would find a way to stop these schools as a practical matter." Taken together the three standards of authoritarianism, puritanism, and religious doctrine define a narrow class of subcultures that may be incapable of undermining public orthodoxy.

The tripartite narrowness of judicial opinions should not obscure the plain fact that the Rudasill case represents progress in enlarging the definition of which subcultures may see their schooling survive the pressure for orthodoxy. The fundamentalist "faith community" is considerably less cohesive and institutionally comprehensive than the Amish community of the 1972 Yoder case. While there are elements of lifestyle that tie Christian fundamentalism together and define some of the separation they claim from the world, the core of the community is not so much institutional structure as it is commonly held values and beliefs. The claim of self-sufficiency the Amish were able to make to demonstrate that their freedom would not impinge upon the resources of the wider society is also considerably weaker for the fundamentalists.

Rudasill moves our thinking about the transmission of culture and the right of dissent closer to a concept of freedom of belief, which might be claimed by any group in the society. *Rudasill* also demonstrates, on a larger scale than did *Yoder,* the lack of convincing evidence that there is a compelling, or even rational, reason for stage regulation of the substance of schooling. Where *Yoder* concerned only the justifications proffered for school attendance above grade eight,

Rudasill involves all twelve grades in its demonstration that professional educators are in too little agreement to provide convincing support for the regulations of state bureaucrats. In spite of this progress toward making freedom of belief equally available to all groups, the net effect of *Rudasill* and all the other cases is likely to remain very limited.

Since these matters must proceed on a case-by-case basis in the absence of legislation, the die is not yet cast. But in the tradition of legal prestidigitation, the courts appear to have taken away with one hand what they have given with the other. If government education bureaucrats in Kentucky do not have the legal power to directly control the transmission of culture in schools, then some other imposed order must be put in its place. Unpredictable, anarchistic, or unruly spirits need not apply. Certainly there is no place for the irreligious. It was Freud who called religion an "illusion" that helps us master feelings of "helplessness in the face of nature's dreaded forces," including our own aggressiveness. But it is the courts that have said that those whose reaction to this helplessness does not include the adoption of one or another of these illusions or the submission to state-sponsored institutions are not likely to invoke the sympathy or the support of the law.

Authoritarianism, puritanism, and Judaeo-Christian religions have thus been defined by the law as part of the official American culture. Groups maintaining these values may be allowed to exist even though they reject other parts of majority culture. Through the courts and the school bureaucracy, the state has served notice of the kinds of dissenting subcultures that will not be permitted to reproduce themselves. Freud summed up the function of this style of regulation as follows:

> The narcissistic satisfaction provided by the cultural ideal is also one of the forces that effectively counteract the hostility to culture within the cultural group. It can be shared not only by the favored classes, which enjoy the benefits of this culture, but also by the suppressed, since the right to

despise those that are outside it compensates them for the wrongs they suffer in their own group. True, one is a miserable plebian, tormented by obligations and military service, but withal one is a Roman citizen, one has one's share in the task of ruling other nations and dictating their laws. This identification of the suppressed with the class that governs and exploits them is, however, only part of a larger whole . . . Unless such relations, fundamentally of a satisfying kind, were in existence, it would be impossible to understand how so many cultures have contrived to exist for so long in spite of the justified hostility of great masses of men.

This is an apt description of subculture survival in general and of the victory of the Kentucky fundamentalists in particular, since they have confined their dissent to a few small areas of belief while identifying with their regulators to a large degree.

Richard Herron is a man who has come to the edge of this dilemma of cultural dissent and personal identification. He is a devoutly religious fundamentalist who, as a "saved" Christian, claims a personal experience of Christ. He is also a sixteen-year veteran officer of the state police. He is a spiritual man, but he is also an authoritarian. When he recalled an earlier service in the military and compared it with the shoddy discipline he perceives now, he observed that he "didn't *like* regimentation but was *proud* of it."

Herron's dilemma was that his commitment to the religion that embodies the spiritual values he needs led him to an act of civil disobedience, which was in complete contradiction to his social role as a law enforcer and his personal tendency to prefer authoritarian structures and behavior. He was told informally that if the court did not uphold his refusal to accept state regulation for the Owensboro Christian Academy, he would lose his job. His decision to take this risk made him "uncomfortable" and "depressed" and he began "to feel like a fanatic." Approaching the limits of his ability to contain the tension between authority and spiritual consciousness, Herron began to develop "a tender place for

184

folks who feel they can readily or rightfully be civilly disobedient," which he admitted might include dissenters of political persuasions and philosophies he did not share. The latent fundamentalist contradiction between personal spirituality and religious authoritarianism was being exposed and played out in Herron's thinking as a conflict between acting on conscience and respecting civil authority.

In the end Herron and the other fundamentalists were able to draw back from a generalized commitment to civil disobedience. The court proceedings effectively handled the matter as a choice between orthodoxies: state sponsored or Christian fundamentalist. The availability of this choice made it possible for Herron to secure his freedom through obedience to an officially approved order of beliefs. But in the process he came very close to seeing that his liberty is a part of the collective liberty and that the striving for freedom of belief cannot be contained by reductionist legal formulas or compendiums of state school regulations. Herron very nearly realized the need to sacrifice his reliance on external authority to attain a higher collective order and a deeper spiritual freedom.

For Herron and those who share his fundamentalist world view, the struggle over state regulation of schooling ended in victory. But the message for other dissenting subcultures is less hopeful. The ideology, professional self-interest, and majority culture embodied in government schooling are all aligned in opposition to the creation or maintenance of dissenting communities. Where those communities are suitably authoritarian, puritanical, and religious, they may enlist the protection of the law; otherwise they are at risk of being cannibalized by it. The structure of schooling and the interpretation of law in the age of majority-controlled education indicate a bleak future for the creation and maintenance of voluntary associations based on beliefs at odds with public orthodoxy.

IV
SEPARATION OF SCHOOL AND STATE

Separation of School and State

By the last quarter of the eighteenth century the political experiences of European and American societies had indicated the importance of a complete separation of church and state. Unless religion and government were confined to separate realms, the political process would be hopelessly factionalized by irreconcilable conflict over spiritual matters, and the freedom of religion of individual citizens would be destroyed by the attempt to substitute religious orthodoxy for legitimate political consensus.

By the last quarter of the twentieth century, nearly two hundred years after the adoption of this principle of separation in the United States Constitution, experience again indicates the cost of building into government a continuing conflict between individual conscience and state-supported orthodoxy. Without a complete separation of school and state, the governing process of American schooling has been increasingly undermined by unresolvable value conflict, and individual freedom of belief, expression, and political participation have been hobbled. Schooling has become a major means of transmitting culture. When government imposes the content of schooling it becomes the same deadening agent of repression from which the framers of the Constitution sought to free themselves.

Public schooling has so often been regarded as the bulwark of democracy and the nation's chief source of social cohesion and equal opportunity that it may seem subversive to suggest that America's school system has become a suppressor of dissent and a manipulator of political consciousness. Moreover, it may be of little comfort to argue—as is done later in this part—that the concept of schooling can be reconceived without endangering the principle of universal, compulsory, public education and without sacrificing the right of equal education opportunity. The difficulty in seeing the present structure of schooling for what it is lies in widely held assumptions about education that cloud public perceptions. It will be difficult to see the effect of schooling structure upon culture and politics if these assumptions are not reexamined and if we are ideologically unwilling to acknowledge the testimony of struggle and resistance given by families whose private beliefs have become public issues.

The conflicts that have been reported here fall into three categories. The first concerns a struggle among families for control of the policies of public schools. These dissenters desire to establish their version of legible and functional values for the socialization of their children but are unable to pursue either private or home education to achieve their goals. They play a zero-sum game in which some values and world views will be stigmatized and others will become school policy. These continuing conflicts over value inculcation in the public schools have become a self-consuming war over the definition of orthodoxy.

A second group of dissenters is of such an individualistic frame of mind that participation in the war over public-school orthodoxy is unthinkable for them. These families seek to avoid the constraints of institutional socialization altogether and to enhance the search for meaning in their lives by educating their children at home. They too have had

190

to spend inordinate amounts of time in barbed, and sometimes vicious, conflict with the agents of government schools.

Finally, there are the efforts of communities or would-be communities to create or maintain a world view and beliefs at odds with majority culture. The desire of these dissenting groups to use private schools as a mechanism for socialization in the interest of cohesiveness has drawn them into long and costly battles with public-education authorities.

One consistent element in all these conflicts is government hostility to dissent and to the educational opportunities that might breed dissent. The hostility exists not on the mundane level of partisan political issues but at the deeper cultural and psychological level of basic values, perceptions, and understandings of life. The families that must deal with this hostility are often the ones that have the greatest energy and concern available for child rearing and are offended by the attitude of apathy and acquiescence upon which institutional schooling so often relies. In part, their engagement defines their dissent. That educators often try to co-opt these issues and make them into questions of pedagogy does not change their meaning for families.

In most ways dissenting families are like the majority. Most parents see the rearing of children as an expression of belief—belief in the children, belief in their own lives, and belief in the future; they feel free to engage in this intimate form of communication as a way of passing along to their children all that is necessary for survival, happiness, and success, however they define them. Dissenting families, however, must pay a heavy price to pursue such natural parental functions and aspirations. To do what the rest of us do with relative ease—perhaps even too much ease—dissenting families have had to seek the approval of state and local school authorities; defend or file costly, time-consuming, and cumbersome lawsuits; risk the loss of jobs, child custody, and family stability; suffer the uncertainty, emotional stress, and personal anxiety of exposing family

191

privacy to official and public scrutiny. For some it has been necessary to fight other families with competing values in order to convince entire blocs of citizens or school officials to enshrine their beliefs in public-school policies. For those who do not adhere to what can only be called public orthodoxy, conflict with the power of the state can become a way of life.

The family that asserts belief, values, world view, or its own peculiar ethics in any of these struggles is a dissenting family, not only because they reject the dominant ethic of majority culture or have been attacked by the bureaucratized agents of that culture but because they seek to create meaning where they perceive only pervasive alienation and voracious skepticism. Whatever the differences of values among these families, they have in common the sense that the assumptions of the majority culture have lost their power of explanation and prediction and that that culture is confused, self-contradicting, or collapsing.

The rational mind may balk at the attempt of some families to substitute ideological commitment, blind faith, or mere groping for a reasoned approach to the complex problems of life, but it cannot be denied that the uncoerced pursuit of meaning is the need of most everyone and the right of all individuals. There is nothing unnatural in asserting one's beliefs and sense of order through child rearing, especially at a time of cultural confusion.

Many dissenting families perceive that in public schools it is the two-dimensional order of bureaucratic rules that often substitutes for a dysfunctional or collapsing cultural consensus. To many parents, government education officials seem to inhabit a world of shifting, arbitrary categories, beset by feuds among bureaucratic baronies and infested with endless insensitivity to individual children and families and with a mindless disregard for the vitality of life.

The institutional education process to which parents are urged to hand over their children may be perceived as advocating secular humanism, classism, sexism, or some other easily labeled attitude. But it is just as likely to be viewed as devoid of any values—as superficial, mindless, and dominated by a commitment to order without ethics. In this context the family that asserts the right to pursue its own beliefs, whether radical or reactionary, asks for meaning where none is wanted by government.

Because these dissenters are engaged in a form of thought and expression that is the common aim of us all and because they seek to employ school socialization as the available, legally prescribed means of forming and transmitting beliefs, it may seem remarkable that they have met with so much resistance from the government. In home-education and private-school cases, this government resistance is produced in part by a contradictory and uncertain education profession, which has bred defensiveness and overreaching in school bureaucrats. But this is at best a partial explanation. At bottom, most of the family/school conflict reviewed here is not resolvable by technical or professional judgments. Instead, these are questions of values, of conscience, of the definition of the good life for which schooling is supposed to be a preparation. In matters of home education and private schooling, professional educators and the political majorities to which they ultimately appealed did not share the values of dissenting families, and these educators used government power to express their disapproval. In the censorship cases the struggle was among competing parental groups, and the aim was control of the government power needed to transform private values into public orthodoxy.

The fact that public-school policy can be used as a means of stigmatizing some beliefs and establishing others means that these struggles do not ultimately serve the purposes of public-school officials or the public. In order to govern, school boards and administrators depend upon the fragile consensus in the local community. But this consensus is weakened by continual strife over values issues. Denying a family the ability to pursue its own educational goals makes the public schools increasingly ungovernable. Were it not for the dependence of most educators upon majority decision making, they might be among the first to perceive that individual liberties are, by definition, exempt from majority control and that nothing is more certain to fragment a community than the public coercion of private decisions.

A few of these value disagreements might have been resolved by a process of mediation or compromise if the power of the parties had been more equal and if the professional educators had been more reasonable about their self-interests. Such possibilities are to be sought, for when conflict resolution is possible, it strengthens the ties of the disputants and the cohesiveness of community. But the vast majority of issues over which the bitter battles of school and family are fought concern irreconcilable world views and matters of personal and cultural identity that are not amenable to compromise or resolution through political processes.

The depth of these world views for the participants is described in the following excerpt from "The Place of Beliefs in Modern Culture" by Murray Murphey:

> . . . Human action at the voluntary level is action guided by belief, appraised and evaluated by norms; without the conceptual systems that provide such beliefs and norms, wants could not be satisfied and effective action would be impossible. The world view is thus the system of beliefs in terms of which human action is planned and executed . . . The world view does more than define what there is and provide a basis for action; it also provides the individual with a set of orientations toward himself and the world around him that are of fundamental significance for his psychological well-being. Without some stability and order in experience and without normative and motivational orientations toward himself, other humans, and his natural environment, the human individual could have no security, no satisfying interpersonal relations, and no moral worth. Who may be loved and who must be hated, what one may be proud of and what one must be ashamed of, who is a friend and who is an enemy—these and hun-

dreds of similar questions are answered for us by the world view. Our ideas can domesticate the world and make us at home there, or they leave us terrified strangers on an alien shore.

(From *New Directions in American Intellectual History*,
Conklin and Higham, Eds., 1979)

As this quotation suggests, the matters of belief, world view, personal conscience, and group identity that often underlie school struggles also have significant political implications. The political opinions that children will express upon achieving majority will be based in part upon the perceptions of the world they absorb in school. The battles between families and school officials for the consciousness of children are, therefore, more than a struggle over the expression of dissenting values in present-day schooling. They are a conflict over the nature of political participation in the future. Public-school officials and the political majorities they claim to represent are engaged in attempts to control the opinions upon which their present and future power depends. For many families the struggle is also related to the future political power of a community or a subgroup.

The issue could be put no more clearly now than it was over a century ago by John Stuart Mill as he looked toward the establishment of compulsory government schooling in *On Liberty*. State-sponsored education, he wrote,

> . . . is a mere contrivance for moulding people to be exactly like one another: and as the mould in which it casts them is that which pleases the predominant power in the government, whether this be a monarch, a priesthood, an aristocracy, or the majority of the existing generation, in proportion as it is efficient and successful, it establishes a despotism over the mind . . .

Another common theme of the cases in which child rearing is the subject of continual conflict concerns the vitality

195

and regenerative ability of both culture and politics. It is clear that the family that dissents from prevailing orthodoxy is subjected to official harassment and loss of basic personal liberties in the name of "the right values" or "good citizenship." But, paradoxically, the cultural and political consensus upon which individual freedoms rest is also a victim of the attempts to create unity in education. Much of the activity that leads dissenting families into conflict with school officials and other agents of the state has its roots in the perception that American cultural assumptions are becoming dysfunctional. Feelings of alienation have fed the growth of efforts by parents to impose some order upon the apparent chaos. The problem for the society at large is that by repressing dissenting values, seeds of future consensus and social cohesion are destroyed. Especially in matters of child rearing and school socialization, the repression of dissenting values is a method of cannibalizing culture.

In the case of home education, for example, government regulation and harassment make it difficult for individual families to explore, create, and pass on beliefs that might become more useful to social survival than public orthodoxy. For subcultures and other groups pursuing community education, government hostility means that the connection between a dissenting world view and a productive life may never be made or demonstrated to the public. Those who believe they have found a better way are prevented from bequeathing it to their children. Finally, among those struggling with each other over public-school policy, the task of creating or passing on personal beliefs requires some families to seek the destruction of competing values held just as sincerely by other families. So mammoth has the requirement of majority control made this task that this avenue for the transmission of cultural alternatives is also effectively closed. As a result, the points at which the culture might regenerate itself become points of destruction. Cut off from these sources of regeneration, an already collapsing culture becomes further ossified and brittle. What might have been a troublesome cultural transition becomes a crisis in which the natural processes of value change are thwarted. Repressive tactics, which have the effect of maintaining a moribund status quo, leave increasing numbers of individuals isolated from supportive communities and at the mercy of state or bureaucratic order.

Dissent developed and expressed in the process of schooling is therefore an important resource for the future growth of culture and the establishment of political consensus. The dead hand of orthodoxy not only deprives substantial numbers of families of the ability to participate in culture and public life, it threatens to end the process of growth altogether and to replace it with what Jung called "the spiritual and moral darkness of State Absolutism." This darkness is one which we are accustomed to thinking about as the condition of totalitarian societies. But perhaps Jung's warning may apply to the ultimate effects of school structure we now praise as democratic. According to Jung:

> The goal and meaning of individual life no longer lie in individual development but in the policy of the State, which is thrust upon the individual from the outside and consists in the execution of an abstract idea which ultimately tends to attract all life to itself. The individual is increasingly deprived of the moral decision as to how he should live his own life, and instead is ruled, fed, clothed and educated as a social unit, and amused in accordance with the standards that give pleasure and satisfaction to the masses . . . State policy decides what shall be taught and studied.

This grim picture does not describe what most families perceive about the functioning of state education officials or the structure of our school system. But it very clearly describes the experiences of families whose dissenting values have brought them into conflict with public school officials or with each other in public-school settings.

197

The First Amendment

These personal, political, and cultural themes emerge from the efforts of families to control their children's education as most families did until this century. But there is another significant lesson to be learned from the struggle between families and schools over the socialization of children—that the present political and financial structure of American schooling is unconstitutional. To date, this pattern and practice of violating basic constitutional rights has been tolerated by the law in all but a few instances because of a flawed understanding of the problem of family/school value conflict. Most judges and legislators have not perceived the centrality of school socialization to the lives of families and the raising of children; neither have they acknowledged the relationship between the formation of world views in children and the expression of opinion protected by the First Amendment. And finally, the courts have been so preoccupied with preventing religious impositions in publicly supported schools that they have virtually ignored the more significant imposition of ideology.

These three flaws in the legal perception of reality have led to judicial errors and problems. The Supreme Court has indirectly approved the role of public schools as including the indoctrination of children with values approved by a majority of the local community. It may be about to directly approve this indoctrination in the Pico case. State and federal courts have permitted government officials to regulate the content of home education and private schooling in the absence of compelling justifications for such regulation. And as Part One indicates, the courts have been unable to apply the First Amendment freedom of expression to censorship cases.

The argument that present school structure is unconstitutional takes as its background the reality of resistance to government-sponsored socialization documented here. It requires the correction of legal misperceptions of this reality;

and it begins with the application of a modern theory of the First Amendment to a government institution all but unknown when the Bill of Rights was adopted.

Government-run schooling, universal, compulsory, and publicly financed has traditionally been viewed by most Americans as an essential democratic institution. According to this view, schooling teaches skills necessary to the exercise of the rights of citizenship, is required for survival in our economic system, and inculcates in the rising generation those values and attitudes that support democratic institutions. In more rapturous, if not historically accurate, moments educators have claimed not only that schooling is the lynchpin of democratic process in America but that the schools are the nation's primary agency for eliminating social ills, inoculating against anti-Americanism, and perfecting the personal and national character.

This equating of the American school system with social democracy and personal liberty may be more self-serving than self-evident. In fact, many recent histories of American education raise the possibility that American schooling may be structured in a way that undercuts the most basic freedoms of democracy. At the heart of American school ideology for the last century has been the belief that schooling decisions, like most governmental decisions, are the proper province of the political majority. The question raised by the families that have been involved in recent conflict with public-school authorities is whether majority control of schooling is compatible with fundamental liberties in general and the First Amendment to the Constitution in particular.

The First Amendment states: "Congress shall make no law respecting an establishment of religion, or prohibiting the free exercise thereof; or abridging the freedom of speech, or of the press; or the right of the people peaceably to assemble, and to petition the Government for a redress of grievances." Although this language was enacted nearly two hundred years ago, it has only been since the First World

199

War that courts have made any substantial effort to apply it. Most theoretical analyses of the First Amendment are therefore relatively recent.

The Amendment contains what may appear to be a disjointed group of rights; and so the search was begun by legal, historical, and political scholars for a core or unifying theme to the Amendment, which would make its application to modern society easier. One such scholar, Alexander Meiklejohn, put the task this way in referring to the intent of the Framers:

> Apparently all they could make their words do was link together five separate demands which had been sharpened by ages of conflict and were being popularly urged in the name of the "freedom of the People." And yet, those demands were, and were felt to be, varied forms of a single demand.

Over a decade later Justice William O. Douglas, history's most committed and insightful interpreter of the First Amendment, pointed out that many rights not specifically enumerated in the Amendment are essential to its function in the constitutional scheme:

> The association of people is not mentioned in the Constitution nor in the Bill of Rights. The right to educate a child in a school of the parents' choice—whether public, private, or parochial—is also not mentioned. Nor is the right to study any particular subject or any foreign language. Yet the First Amendment has been construed to include certain of these rights . . . In other words, the state may not, consistent with the spirit of the First Amendment, contract the spectrum of available knowledge. The right of freedom of speech and press includes not only the right to utter or print, but the right to distribute, the right to receive, the right to read, and freedom of inquiry, freedom of thought, freedom to teach . . . Without these peripheral rights the specific rights would be less secure.

200

The "peripheral" rights and the specific, enumerated rights thus have a unifying theme, and understanding the unifying theme of the First Amendment is a necessary first step for the task of applying it to universal schooling. One of the most comprehensive and thoughtful examinations of the First Amendment comes from Professor Thomas I. Emerson of Yale Law School, once a pupil of Justice Douglas, in *Toward a General Theory of the First Amendment* (1969):

> The values sought by society in protecting the right to freedom of expression may be grouped into four broad categories. Maintenance of a system of free expression is necessary (1) as a method of assuring individual self-fulfillment, (2) as a means of attaining the truth, (3) as a method of securing participation by the members of the society in social, including political, decision-making, and (4) as a means of maintaining the balance between stability and change in society.

The inclusion of self-fulfillment means that in Emerson's view of the First Amendment the individual is not only the basis of the political structure, he or she is the basis of society: "Every man—in the development of his own personality—has the right to form his own beliefs and opinions. Hence, suppression of belief, opinion and expression is an affront to the dignity of man, a negation of man's essential nature."

Emerson reflects the basic importance that culture and the Constitution place upon the unfettered development of human personality. By this theory, holding beliefs and expressing them are worthwhile in themselves, without reference to political or public justifications. Emerson also saw that "belief is the starting point of all other rights," so that even though belief is not identical to expression, the system of freedom of expression protected by the First Amendment could not operate without freedom of belief. This same intimate connection of freedom of belief and expression with human nature was expressed even more forcefully by Paolo Freire in *Pedagogy of the Oppressed*: "Men . . . cannot be

201

truly human apart from communication, for they are essentially communicative creatures. To impede communication is to reduce men to the status of 'things' . . ."

The quintessential importance of individual human development is reflected by Justice Douglas's dissent from the Court's opinion in a conscientious objector case. "I had assumed," he wrote, "that the welfare of a single human soul was the ultimate test of the vitality of the First Amendment." These conceptions of the First Amendment touch a central function of the schoolroom, where communication, belief, and human development are focused six hours a day.

If the First Amendment was meant to protect the sanctity of human personality and its development from government coercion, it is no less designed as a protection for the political individual. This politically centered theory of the core meaning of the First Amendment was most completely articulated by Alexander Meiklejohn who wrote that "the revolutionary intent of the First Amendment is . . . to deny all subordinate agencies authority to abridge the freedom of the electoral power of the people."

Meiklejohn's theory is that the Amendment is concerned not simply with the freedom to speak or print or believe but with the whole range of activities of thought and communication involved in government by the people. The theory simultaneously expands the coverage of the First Amendment (to include all forms of expression, intellect, and knowledge) and contracts its intent (to include only activities related to governing and the sovereignty of the people). The political individual, alone or in voluntary association, is seen as the basis of the governing process, with the Constitution as an individualist document conveying only limited powers to government and resting its entire structure upon the just consent of the governed. The formulation and expression of this consent is what is protected by the First Amendment, and any exercise of freedom of expression is protected from government abridgement "whenever those activities are utilized for the governing of the nation." Meiklejohn's enumeration of the freedoms necessarily related to the exercise of the governing power under the First Amendment is expansive and includes not only "spreading information and opinions" but "creating knowledge and understanding," and "education in all its phases." Most pointedly for school problems, Meiklejohn's conception of the unifying theme of diverse First Amendment rights means that no regulation of belief can be tolerated:

> A citizen may be told when and where and in what manner he may or may not speak, write, assemble, and so on. On the other hand, he may not be told what he shall or shall not believe. In that realm, each citizen is sovereign.

The logic of Meiklejohn's formulation suggests that government control of content in the education of a captive audience is tantamount to infringement of the individual's governing powers. Schooling, as dissenting families have testified, is among the most sensitive points in transmission of beliefs. The society that utilizes the institutional power of involuntary schooling to reduce an individual's control over the development of personal conscience and consciousness threatens to make that individual politically impotent. Under these conditions the government becomes a kind of political perpetual-motion machine, legitimizing its long-term policies through the world view and public opinion it creates.

Taken together, Emerson, Meiklejohn, Douglas, and others who have sought the central theme of the First Amendment's many rights reveal a conception of the individual as the central unit of political and social being, free to develop in his own way, to express himself, and to engage in the struggle to mold social institutions, culture, and public policy without government interference. The First Amendment is thus a statement of the dignity and worth of every individual. The particular freedoms of the Amendment are part of a system that guarantees individual and group expression and insures that opinions and beliefs are freely given and exchanged in a marketplace of ideas. Self-expression—

which is an end in itself; community building—a voluntary process that sustains and defines the self; and the fair and reliable making of public policy are all served by the specific First Amendment protections.

The question becomes how to apply the First Amendment to compulsory public schooling—an institution all but unknown when the Amendment was written. On the surface this has not been a difficult task. In legal opinions it is commonplace to recognize that schools, as institutions occupying a substantial portion of a child's waking life, ought to respect the First Amendment rights of students and teachers. The law has recognized that students and teachers "do not shed their constitutional rights to freedom of speech or expression at the schoolhouse gate." The right to publish controversial articles in student newspapers or to symbolically express political opinions has been upheld, as have teachers' rights to hold and express opinions or join political organizations without fear of reprisal by school officials. But these are responses to specific restrictions on freedom of press, speech, or association imposed by school authorities and are more properly recognized as the most obvious and superficial examples of restrictions on First Amendment rights imbedded in schooling. These examples barely scratch the surface of value inculcation as it takes place in school.

To apply the First Amendment to schooling requires acknowledging the inevitability and the depth of this value inculcation. The struggles of these families are replete with evidence of how overt and hidden curriculums affect the transmission of culture and the formation of world view in schools. The role models teachers provide, the structure of classrooms and of teacher-student relationships, the way in which the school is governed, the textbooks that are approved, the concepts that are tested for, the attitudes and behavior that are rewarded or punished—all convey messages about approved and rewarded values and beliefs. Parents who oppose school authorities on issues of home education, private-school standards, or the content of curriculum and library know that schooling is not value free. Scholars who have studied the process of pedagogy and the function of education know that schooling cannot be made value free. And teachers who have labored at making connections between teaching and learning know that to try to make schooling value free is to destroy the purpose of education.

As the struggles of dissenting families also show, the fundamental relationship between school socialization and the First Amendment has not been addressed in a forthright and systematic manner by either the courts or civil-liberties lawyers. Up until recently, in fact, the effect of many of the Supreme Court's schooling cases has been to uphold and entrench the legal fiction that schooling can be value neutral. By the frequent use of a dichotomy between secular and religious education, the Court has been able to eliminate an obvious form of belief manipulation—religious observance—from public schools. But it has thereby implied that the secular content of schooling does not touch upon the basic beliefs and world views of students or that such beliefs are unworthy of constitutional protection. More recently the Court has implied a shift from equating secularism with neutrality to viewing the inculcation of secular values in school as consistent with individual freedom so long as they are majority values that are forced upon students. If such statist thinking were to leave the realm of *obiter dictum* and find its way into the Court's doctrine, it would fly in the face of every known conception of individual liberty and First Amendment freedom. Resisting such an eventuality depends in part upon having a clear and practical conception of how the First Amendment can be applied to school socialization without destroying either of them.

To apply the First Amendment to school socialization is to broaden the Amendment's traditional protection of *expression* of belief and opinion to embrace the *formation* of belief and opinion.

In fact, the connection between expression and formation of beliefs is so close they are nearly inseparable. Freedom of expression makes possible the unfettered formulation of belief and opinion in an atmosphere of open exchange uncon-stricted by government. In turn, the governmentally un-coerced formulation of beliefs and opinions is essential to freedom of expression. If the government were able to use schooling to regulate the development of ideas and opinions by controlling the transmission of culture and the socializa-tion of children, freedom of expression would become a meaningless right; just as government control of expression would make the formation of belief and opinion a state-dominated rather than an individually based process. If the First Amendment protected only the communication and not the formation of ideas, totalitarianism and freedom of ex-pression could be characteristics of the same society. In modern times the opportunity to coerce consciousness pre-cedes, and may do away with, the need to manipulate ex-pression.

Although an understanding of the First Amendment and schooling begins with a recognition of the specific freedoms of expression, it ultimately involves the capacity to be hu-man, the ability to participate in political action and to ac-quire and produce knowledge, and the ability to transform such knowledge into power that affects the conditions of daily life. In a society dependent on institutional child rear-ing, it is on schooling that these activities have their greatest impact.

The expression/formation connection between the First Amendment's emphasis on the dignity of the individual and education's inevitable influence on personal development and transmission of culture suggests a formulation of First Amendment principles as follows: the development as well as the expression of those beliefs, opinions, world views, and aspects of conscience that constitute individual con-sciousness should be free of government coercion through schooling.

The consequences of applying this First Amendment principle to the present structure of schooling are clear. Eliminating family educational choice or permitting gov-ernment regulation of content of schooling renders individual expression, self-fulfillment, and personal development meaningless. So long as individual dignity matters, the individual ought to control his own education; where the individual is too young to make an informed and voluntary choice, his parents ought to control it.

The same First Amendment principle indicates that if the effect of lack of school choice on individual liberty is important, more important still is the effect that government-sponsored coercion of consciousness has upon the political process and the political sovereignty of the individual. Coercive socialization in public schools or publicly regulated schools—even socialization according to the values of the community majority—affects world views and therefore distorts political action. If the most sensitive point in the transmission of beliefs and the definition of knowledge were not protected by the First Amendment, an originating point of the consent of the governed would be controlled by the government, and all communication, learning, speech, voting, and assembling would be colored and distorted by this coercive tampering with individual consciousness.

Thus the First Amendment's concern for the formation of individual belief and for individual self-fulfillment in schooling is joined to a concern for the exercise of individual political sovereignty and the legitimate formation of political majorities. Though it is not immediately effective, there is a strong connection between the world views children are rewarded for adopting in school and their political activities and opinions as adults. The war over orthodoxy has political consequences.

A democratic process for the formulation of public policy can be preserved only if no group or political majority can use school socialization to maintain or extend its ideology or political power. Yet much of the conflict over schooling has just these political overtones and motivations. When the effect of majority control of socialization is to prevent some students from acquiring the ability to make themselves heard politically or to distort the participation in public affairs of students when they become adults, they will find themselves the victims of others who are better able to understand and express their own interests or their personal visions of the general welfare.

The law has not waited for this articulation of modern First Amendment theory to recognize the importance of protecting individual development and the healthy functioning of the political system from the dead hand of the state. In 1922 Oregon passed legislation banning private schools. When this Ku Klux Klan-inspired bit of jingoism reached the Supreme Court, it was declared unconstitutional, and the justices offered their opinion in *Pierce* v. *Society of Sisters* that "the child is not the mere creature of the state." In the Court's words, the "fundamental theory of liberty excludes any general power of the state to standardize its children by forcing them to accept instruction from public teachers only." The right of families to attend nongovernment schools in satisfaction of the compulsory education laws was thus affirmed, but the Court also implied that states could make reasonable regulations of private schools.

The *Pierce* decision has been reaffirmed numerous times regardless of whether the private school is secular or sectarian, but the extent to which these schools can be regulated by the state has remained unclear. Shortly after the landmark *Pierce* decision, the Court did hold that the right to attend an alternative to government-controlled schools could not be obliterated by a scheme of regulation of private schools so detailed that the differences between government and private schools became insignificant. As the struggles of some dissenting families have shown, the point at which state regulation of private schooling crosses the line of constitutional permissibility has remained ill marked. This is due in part to the Court's failure to address the First Amendment consequences of government control of the value content of schooling.

Whatever the shortcomings of the legal conception of what is at stake in school conflicts, the courts have reiterated time and again the general principle that government control of socialization through schooling cannot be used to foster "a

208

homogeneous people with American ideals," or to make the child "the mere creature of the state."

One of the strongest statements of this protection of the private nature of belief formation came in the 1943 case of *West Virginia* v. *Barnette,* involving the pledge of allegiance. A state statute compelling public-school students to salute the flag each day was declared invalid under the First Amendment as a form of utterance that required "affirmation of a belief and attitude of mind." In the words of Justice Robert Jackson, "If there is any fixed star in our constitutional constellation, it is that no official, high or petty, can prescribe what shall be orthodox in politics, nationalism, religion, or other matters of opinion or force citizens to confess by word or act their faith therein." Such confessions by word or act are the stuff of daily activity in schools, but the Court has forbidden only the most overt and obvious value inculcation in schools or has restricted its protection of children and families from government coercion to instances involving religious values.

It is essential to understanding many modern school conflicts to recognize that many of the cases curbing government power of value inculcation in schools rested not only upon the liberty of families in child rearing and the dignity of individual self-development but upon the prevention of unmanageable conflict over matters of conscience. In *Barnette,* for example, Justice Jackson pointed out that the governance of schools and the stability of society would be permanently disrupted by "finding it necessary to choose what doctrine and whose program public educational officials shall compel youth to unite in embracing." Had Justice Jackson been presented with a sophisticated challenge to the pervasive inculcation of values by political majorities controlling schools, he might have recognized an invasion of "the sphere of intellect and spirit" similar to the compulsory flag salute. Certainly he predicted the continual struggle of dissenting families to protect their own beliefs and world views when he wrote about public education that "if it is to impose any ideological discipline, however, each party or

209

denomination must seek to control, or failing that, to weaken the influence of the educational system."

The entire argument about First Amendment consequences of schooling and the constitutional protection of the right to choose a meaningful alternative to government schools might simply prove that a majoritarian school system is consistent with the tenets of political democracy and individual dignity. As long as it provides that dissenting families may send their children to private schools or make use of home instruction, the present structure of compulsory schooling should be seen as violating no important constitutional or political rights. But to arrive at such a conclusion would be to ignore the import of conflicts between families and school authorities reported here as well as the economic structure of our school system.

One of the most obvious conclusions to be drawn from a review of school/family conflict is that government policy and action are hostile to dissent in education. The authorities charged with overseeing nongovernment schools and home education could hardly have made these educational efforts more difficult if they had simply banned them. For whatever reasons of professional preservation, ideological disagreement, or paternalistic concern for children, most public-school officials neither understood nor supported the right of families to pursue education for their children according to the family's own beliefs.

When government power can be used in this way, without substantial constitutional restraints being imposed, the right to an alternative to government schools becomes less and less significant. With the right of choice so restricted, claiming that a dissenting family need not concern itself with value inculcation in government schools because alternatives are legally available is inviting the dissenter to pick his poison. In order to offer a real escape from government-coerced socialization, the First Amendment significance of school choice would have to be recognized, and alternatives to government schools would have to be constitutionally protected from content regulation except where compelling state interests exist.

Even with such constitutional protections for real educational diversity, however, most families remain too poor and overworked to make use of private schools or home education. These families, in Justice Jackson's prophetic words, "must seek to control, or failing that, to weaken the educational system." They become the parents who seek to censor government-school curriculum or libraries and whose desperate desire for comprehensible culture makes them the advocates of firing teachers and burning books. And if a family's sense of personal restraint prevents it from doing battle with neighbors over whose values shall become public-school orthodoxy, the reward may be to endure in apathy or in silent anger as their children become alienated and confused by the cultural vacuum of government schooling. In spite of the escape-valve theory of alternatives to government education, the right of educational choice remains a prerogative of the wealthy.

We have created a system of school finance that provides free choice for the rich and compulsory socialization for everyone else. The present method of financing American education discriminates against the poor and the working class and even a large part of the middle class by conditioning the exercise of First Amendment rights of school choice upon an ability to pay while simultaneously eroding the ability to pay through the regressive collection of taxes used exclusively for government schools. This arrangement seems no more defensible than denying the right to vote to those who cannot afford a poll tax.

The present method of financing schooling in America is neither accidental nor immutable. It can be changed to provide real family choice in schooling without destroying the system of compulsory education or undercutting equal education opportunity. At present we allow the majority to dictate what values school children will learn in government schools *and* what the alternatives to those schools will be. To

211

support this process we collect tax money from every citizen, yet do not permit the dissenting family to have the advantage of those dollars. The family that does not wish to have its children internalize a set of values it finds abhorrent or suffer the conflict and alienation that result from competing efforts to control the children's learning must pay private-school tuition as well as public-school tax. In effect, this system confronts the dissenting family with a choice between giving up its basic values and beliefs as the price of gaining a "free" education in a government school or paying twice in order to preserve its First Amendment rights.

Naturally, the burden of forced choices between economic survival and the preservation of personal and cultural values falls most heavily upon the poor, the working class, and those minorities that are overrepresented in that segment of society. One would imagine that the right to create and maintain dissenting world views and beliefs would be no more important to any group than to those who are continuously short-changed by the dominant ethic. Yet while these people are deprived of personal or subcultural control over education, our present school ideology tells them that the present structure of schooling is their best hope for an equal place in society. The result is that those who are least able to resist are systematically deprived of their ability to dissent in the molding of their children's minds.

Rectifying this situation requires recognizing that liberty in education must be made available to all families or it is meaningful to none. More to the point, it requires the rearranging of the present method of financing public schooling so that it no longer discriminates against the choices of the nonwealthy. Such a reconstruction would be based upon the individual's right to be free of government coercion where the formation of beliefs and conscience are at stake. Wherever beliefs, world views, values, or ideologies are at stake, the Constitution must be read to impose the same government neutrality as is brought into play with regard to religion. If the First Amendment is applied to the reality of schooling as it has developed in this century, the conclusion must be that individual liberty, the healthy functioning of the political system, and the preservation of a truly public and governable public-school system require a separation of school and state.

To create a separation of school and state and to establish government neutrality in place of the current ideological favoritism requires insuring the reality of school choice for all families and prohibiting local, state, or federal governments from regulating the content of nongovernment schooling, directly or indirectly, except where compelling justifications exist. "Compelling justifications" is a legal term of art that does not include most of the reasons given by school bureaucrats for denying permission for home education, for controlling some aspect of private schooling, or for censoring books and curriculums in government schools. The term does not include the pedagogical preferences of government educators; the values subscribed to by the political majority as patriotic, healthy, or admirable; religious preferences; styles of learning; definitions of the good life; epistemology; or the fear of "smut." Compelling justifications for overriding the First Amendment right to be free of government coercion of conscience and belief in schools must be of such magnitude and widespread public importance—as for example the prevention of epidemics—that they can properly be regarded as more important than fundamental liberties. Imposing this well-established constitutional standard on government bodies that attempt to regulate the essentially private function of education would eliminate upwards of 95 percent of the conflicts over schooling reported here.

The argument for separation of school and state cannot be complete without referring to that justification for government regulation that is most clearly compelling: the struggle against racism in schooling. It is compelling because of the long and brutal history of race in America and because of the established meaning of the Thirteenth, Fourteenth, and Fifteenth Amendments to the Constitution. Among all the

213

choices the First Amendment entitles individuals and families to make in satisfying the compulsory education laws, discrimination on the basis of race is not included.

To argue for liberty in schooling without examining whether that liberty is available regardless of race would be to pretend that America's most enduring and corrosive cultural problem does not exist. In separating school and state, a refusal to create stringent protections against race discrimination in school admissions, programs, curriculum, and distribution of benefits would be to place the entire power of government behind the institutionalization of private discrimination. It is an effort that has been made for years under the banner of parental liberty. But the lesson of the past twenty-five years of resistance to school desegregation is that no plan of private schooling, tax credits, tax deductions, tuition vouchers, or scholarships, which has either the intent or the effect of promoting racial discrimination, can be constitutionally tolerated. It must be seen that racial minorities are among those who have most systematically been denied the educational liberty, which, it is argued here, is the birthright of all.

The Politics of Unequal Liberty

For the past decade the nation has been awash in proposals claiming to expand family choice in education—tuition tax credits, direct aid to private schools, and tuition vouchers of every possible technical design and political effect. These proposals have been the subjects of government studies, scholarly analysis, legislative hearings, and interest-group politics. It has not been the purpose of this book to comment on these proposals but, rather, to describe the causes of school conflict and to analyze the consequences of a system of education that undercuts some of our most important freedoms.

This description of how the political and financial structure of American schooling compels belief and constricts liberty would not be complete without a brief evaluation of at least one of the most widely discussed proposals for increased choice in education. The evaluation is meant to present the practical side to a concern for freedom of belief in America's schools.

On November 3, 1981, the voters of Washington, D.C., defeated the "Greater Educational Opportunities Through Tax Incentives" initiative by a two to one margin. The tax-credit plan was described in brief by its advocates as follows:

> Provides District of Columbia income tax credit for taxpayers who pay educational expenses on behalf of District of Columbia residents in full-time attendance at public or private schools which maintain racially nondiscriminatory policies, enrollment at which complies with the Compulsory School Attendance Laws. Limits credit to $1200 per pupil for tax year ending December 31, 1982, with provisions for annual increases thereafter. Limits total credit to the amount of income tax payable for individual taxpayers; limits credit to 50% of income tax payable for other taxpayers, including corporations.

The language of the proposed initiative indicates that the $1,200 per pupil tax credit (i.e., reduction in taxes owed) would be available for tuition and other educational fees actually charged by private or public educational institutions through grade twelve. Although public schools are in general prohibited by law from charging tuition, any "educational fees," such as lab or trip fees, books, or sports participation fees, charged by public schools would presumably result in a tax credit for those paying these bills.

The tax credits are limited by the amount of tax actually owed by the person claiming the credit so that a person whose tax liability is only $400 for the year cannot receive the benefit of the remaining $800 in credits even if that taxpayer in fact paid a $1,200 tuition bill for a pupil. Eligibility for the tax credit is not limited to parents or guardians of the pupil incurring the educational expenses. Other taxpayers such as relatives, friends, or wealthy individuals who actually pay the educational fees of an eligible student can claim the credit, as can corporations, partnerships, or associations. The credit for corporations, partnerships, and associations is limited to 50 percent of their income tax in any one year.

Attendance at any public or private school that meets the compulsory attendance requirements qualifies a student's actual educational expenses for a tax credit. The only other restriction on the use of the credit is that the school attended maintain "racially non-discriminatory policies as required by law." The $1,200 credit could be increased each year by the D.C. Council to account for inflation. The proposed tuition tax credit plan is substantially the same as one now being circulated in California as a state constitutional amendment.

The plan raises substantial issues about separation of church and state that might eventually result in its being declared unconstitutional. Any proposal resulting in a more equitable funding mechanism for private schooling would raise such questions. But the broader issue of intellectual freedom and family choice in education must be of primary concern here. From the perspective of families struggling to achieve independence from government compulsion of belief in schools, the D.C. Greater Educational Opportunities Through Tax Incentives design must be regarded as unsatisfactory and counterproductive for three reasons:

1. *Parental power.* Twelve hundred dollars per student might conceivably be enough to increase the number of families that can choose freely from among offered public and private schools; but the primary victims of value coercion in schools are those at the bottom rungs of the economic ladder whose tax liabilities come nowhere near $1,200 per child per year. Analyzing a similar plan for California, Professors John Coons and Stephen Sugarman estimated that a family with an income of $20,000 per year would owe less than $440 in state taxes. Working class and poor families would have the benefit not of $1,200 per child but of as little as $200 per child. A family of four will therefore be at a continuing dis-

216

advantage in the attempt to purchase education suitable to its own values.

The D.C. plan apparently tried to remedy the problem of a school finance plan that discriminates in favor of the wealthy by permitting relatives, wealthy individuals, and corporations to take substantial tax credits for funds paid to schools for the "qualified educational expenses" of individual students. The theory is apparently that those who can benefit from tax credits will perform acts of charity for those who cannot use the tax credit. The reality of such a proposal, however, is that those who have traditionally been kept from exercising educational choice by the economic structure of schooling will wind up with even less power over their children's education than they now have. Families with modest or low incomes will become supplicants to the wealthy or to corporations, seeking the payment of educational expenses by the wealthy but discovering that payments are made to the schools or under conditions that please the contributor rather than the family. Instead of being required to sacrifice the right to influence value formation in their children as a condition of receiving a "free" public education, these parents will be asked to make the same sacrifice as a condition of receiving scholarship aid at a private school. Those schools or students that do not share the values of the wealthy simply will lack support.

Where parents have now only the minor influence of voting about public-school policy, they would, under the proposed tax-credit plan, have no influence whatsoever. Put in terms of its overall economic consequences, the credit-for-contribution plan will transfer the control of millions of dollars of school funds from a disputatious majority to an economic elite. Educational liberty will remain a frustrated dream for those who are the current victims of its absence in the government school system. The fact that the $1,200 tax credit would not be rebatable and that the wealthy can continue to price the poor out of the school market effectively disenfranchises most families from deciding about their children's schooling.

217

2. *Race*. Racial minorities, along with the nonwealthy, constitute the group most systematically deprived of liberty in schooling under current conditions. The D.C. tax-credit plan provided some protection against freedom of choice becoming a pretext for racial discrimination, in requiring that schools for which tax credits can be earned have racially nondiscriminatory policies "as required by law." But such protection is insufficient, if not disingenuous. Given the propensity of government to alter the law—especially the tax law—by regulatory manipulation, the lack of adequate protection in the D.C. plan against racial discrimination is fatal.

The tax-credit proposal contains no definitions of what constitutes race discrimination. It does not indicate, for example, whether testing, tracking, and disciplinary policies as well as admission policies are covered by the prohibition of discrimination. It contains no statement that racial equality in all phases of schooling constitutes a compelling interest of overwhelming importance, even where religious reasons for discrimination are advanced. It does not enumerate which laws are "applicable" to the schools attended under the tax-credit plan, though it defines the credits as not being "government financial assistance," a definition that would seem to make some federal antidiscrimination laws inapplicable.

Worse still, the proposal's expressed concern for preventing racial discrimination has no teeth. How will racial discrimination be addressed in a school attended by pupils for whom tax credits are claimed? Who can file a complaint about the discriminatory practices? Will all tax credits for students at that school be denied if discrimination is proved? By what standard will discrimination be judged to have been proved? Since freedom-of-choice plans in schooling over the last twenty-five years have a history of being designed to restrict educational freedom for blacks and other minorities while enhancing it for whites, the absence of adequate protections in the D.C. tax-credit proposal should be enough in itself to disqualify it from public support.

3. *Government control of school content.* One of the lessons to be learned from the struggles of families who are able to afford nongovernment schools is that these schools are not automatically safe havens from government attempts at value coercion. One of the chief mechanisms by which home education and private schools have been subjected to government controls in the absence of compelling justifications has been through equivalency requirements. Often the alternative school is required to meet a vague standard of equivalency to government schools in order to qualify under the compulsory attendance law. While many state compulsory attendance laws contain only minimal requirements, the war over censorship suggests that the field is open for additional requirements fashioned to suit prevailing political majorities. Moreover, the term "equivalence" has been read to permit even the most idiosyncratic standards to be applied by public-school officials against their competitors.

The D.C. tax-credit proposal imposed no additional content requirements on schools as part of the tax-credit plan. It even "presumes" that private schools meet the minimum standards applicable to all schools in the District of Columbia. But this presumption only operates "provided the instruction, quality of education, ethics, health and safety, and fiscal responsibility are *substantially equivalent* to the standard maintained in public schools in the District of Columbia" (emphasis added). Thus is the control of schooling content, which the D.C. proposal claims to put in the hands of individual families, returned to those who control government schools.

It is doubtful whether the D.C. tax-credit proposal as written and as defeated by the voters would have substantially increased the parental liberty of any but those who already had the wherewithal to purchase their freedom. The proposal might easily be rewritten to remedy these problems; but as it stood in November of 1981, this plan promised more, rather than less, coercion of belief for the very

219

same people whose intellectual freedom is now most stifled by the schools.

The foregoing evaluation of one plan for increased family liberty and the analysis of family/school conflicts suggest three broad questions to be addressed in considering the merits of any proposed restructuring of American education.

1.   Would the new structure remove economic discrimination in the choice of schools and prevent some families from pricing others completely out of the market, thereby becoming truly voluntary for families complying with compulsory education requirements?

2.   Would the new structure provide a clear and enforceable policy that race discrimination in any form and in any aspect of schooling is illegal?

3.   Would the new structure protect individuals, families, and schools from government manipulation of beliefs and world views? Is the direct or indirect regulation of family choice or school content prohibited except where compelling justifications exist?

When these issues can be acknowledged as part of the political debate over schooling, dissenting families can receive public thanks instead of government harassment for what they have taught us—that the present structure of education in America is broadly inconsistent with First Amendment principles. This inconsistency, which reflects the contradiction between majoritarian control of schooling and freedom of belief, amounts to a taxation on dissent levied against those to whom dissent is most important—the poor, the working class, and ethnic minorities.

The burden on dissent, which results from failure to make educational liberty available to all families, becomes heavier and more painful at a time in which cultural explanations are losing power, and people are more in need of open communication and the freedom to develop functional world views than they are of repressive enforcement of bureaucratic order or outworn orthodoxy. The question of educational choice is transformed by the times into the question of what structure of schooling is most likely to survive a cultural crisis, and least likely to undermine freedom of intellect and spirit.

Index

227